rivers of a wounded heart

A Capital Discoveries Book, a series that features journeys of self-discovery, transformation, inner-awareness, and recovery. Other titles include:

Reading Water by Rebecca Lawton
Ancient Wisdom: A Chinese Calligrapher's Tale by P. Zbar
There's a Porcupine in My Outhouse by Michael J. Tougias
My Renaissance: A Widow's Healing Pilgrimage to Tuscany by Rose Marie Curteman
Wise Women Speak to the Woman Turning 30 by Jean Aziz and Peggy Stout
Midlifeman: A Book for Guys and the Women Who Want to Understand Them by Larry Krotz
Touching Quiet: Reflections in Solitude by Mindy Weisel
Daughters of Absence: Transforming a Legacy of Loss by Mindy Weisel
Letting Your Heart Sing: A Daily Journal for the Soul by Deborah Tyler Blais

rivers of a wounded heart

every man's journey

michael wilbur

A Capital Discoveries Book

CAPITAL
BOOKS, INC.
Sterling, Virginia

Capital Books, Inc.
P.O. Box 605
Herndon, Virginia 20172-0605

Library of Congress Cataloging-in-Publication Data

Wilbur, Michael.
Rivers of a wounded heart : every man's journey / Michael Wilbur.—1st ed.
p. cm.
ISBN 1-892123-58-4 (alk. paper)
1. Psychotherapists—Biography. 2. Psychotherapy patients—Case studies. I. Title.

RC480.8 .W54 2002
616.89'14'092—dc21
[B]
2001058160

Printed in the United States of America on acid-free paper that meets the American National Standards Institute Z39-48 Standard.

First Edition

10 9 8 7 6 5 4 3 2 1

Dedication

For Janice there are not enough words . . . not enough words, or not the words that I can find to adequately tell you about our love, our relationship, our time together, her, the meaning she has given to me and gives to my life. Some of the stories in *Rivers* may help to better describe and explain my feelings toward Janice and my love for her. The more important element, though, is that she knows my feelings, my thoughts, and my heart—with and without words. Broken hearts do heal, pretty lady; you gotta believe that for me.

For Ross, my son, I love that you now call me Old Man (Edutsi). It took us some time to get to this place in our lives together, but the journey has been worth the wounds to our hearts. You give me the faith and spirit to believe that even though stepping away is sometimes necessary, it should not be the final step with someone you truly, truly love in your heart. I know you will take me with you when I leave, Rossi, as I will you—always. If I could ask God one thing, I would ask Him to stop the moon in the sky so this day would last forever.

For Cathy who, like her mother, Janice, loves me with all my limitations and faults and is, of her three children, the most like Janice in appearance, spirit, personality, intelligence, energy, excitement about life, sensitivity, acceptance, and caring. If Janice and I had had a daughter together, she would have been Cathy.

For Christine, whose wedding (which took place on glistening snow in the sun-cast, shadow peaks of the Grand Teton Mountains near Jackson Hole, Wyoming) I did not attend. Chris was married on March 23, 2002, and, for reasons she knows and understands, I was not with her—physically. In heart, mind, and soul, however, I was no place other than with her on that day. Christine's connection to others is through nature: the sun, the wind, the snow, the water. Chris often strikes me as lonely, but she finds balance and stability in her life by distancing herself from that which is harmful and connecting to others by creating and preserving things in our environment. What better way is there to connect with one's own heart, mind, and spirit, and those of others?

For Jonathan, our oldest son, with whom Janice and I had no contact for over eight years (from 1993 to 2001), who reentered our lives recently as if he—and we—were never apart from the other. The reasons for our estrangement no longer seem important; what is more important is our reconnection in a manner that continues our relationship where we left off—there is no need to rehash the past. All my life's a circle—it's the "nature" of crisscrossing rivers and the healing, nurturing force of their everlasting relationship to one another's lives.

For Edil, my student, colleague, friend, and adopted son of sorts—I'm not sure who adopted whom first—who still sees me as his mentor and I hope, selfishly, that he always will in some way. Edil has always been there for me and always will be. When he loves you, his loyalty and commitment to you are forever.

For Jim, my eccentric best male-friend, the only man who ever rubbed my feet. It was during a time of crisis, sadness, illness, and darkness, with him standing at the end of my bed and tears in his eyes, that he gently rubbed the lotion on my swollen feet and legs when I needed his touch more than any words he could say to me. I may need that from him again one day. We sailed together that next summer as he said we would.

For Michael whom I met in the desert of Arizona and where I became his uncle and he became my nephew–family. Such a wise heart for such a young man; he touched my heart on first meeting. His Eagle spirit from the land beneath the rising sun, and from the Medicine Bag, gives the Bear in me the strength to heal and venture from my cave, still searching for the Eagle in me.

For Rollie, Roland, my father, whom I wish I had had more time with after we healed the wounds to each other's hearts and before he died. I took him with me, though, in my heart. I have never missed the estrangement and anguish between us, just him.

Contents

Foreword

Consider yourself fortunate having this book in your hand, ready to dive in. You are in for a powerful and enriching experience.

The title, *Rivers of a Wounded Heart,* gives us a preview of what to expect. Water is a key element in Wilbur's world: "I sense that people, their lives and relationships are like rivers. . . . Like rivers, our merging and joining with others may be calming, cleansing, and healing, but it also may be raging or toxic, powerfully overwhelming."

From his early childhood experiences growing up near a fascinating but dangerous river to a recent exploration of the fascination and danger of ocean sailing, Wilbur presents both his literal encounters with water and his appreciation of water as a metaphor for human life. This understanding is enriched by the insightful comment of his life companion, Janice, who says, "The cure for anything is saltwater; sweat, tears, or the sea."

He speaks from the heart, another key word in his title and in his life. You encounter here not the polished pretty predictable presentation of an orderly serene life in which personal issues are solved, relationships are enduring, and difficulties are easily overcome. Instead you encounter a man of flesh and blood, who is immersed in the struggles and conflicts of human life. What you encounter is not a set of cheap platitudes from an easy life, but a genuine sense of the pain and pleasure of living life to its fullest. It is a book which comes to you from the heart.

And the heart that speaks is a wounded heart. From the pain of growing up with a father who was the town drunk, to the searing pain of losing his son through a divorce, to his ongoing struggle to teach with integrity, one comes to feel what it has cost Wilbur to live his life. His title for one chapter is "Barn's Burnt Down . . . Now I Can See the Moon." This wonderfully poignant statement is an apt description of Wilbur's life. Although he has suffered many losses, he finds a way to see beyond them to the enduring gifts of life.

He quotes an inscription on the back of a photograph from a former student and Vietnam combat veteran, who says, "I cannot bring you detachment's gift of casual reason; I've only my heart's emotion and deep, gentle sadness to give to you." It is this same heart's emotion and deep, gentle sadness that the author shares with us, his readers.

But the wounded heart is also a heart that rejoices. Amid the darkness are flashes of light and incredible sunrises. The cost of living a full, unprotected life is the pain one inevitably encounters; the satisfaction in living such a life is in the intensity of its moments of joy and accomplishment.

There are lovely reflections on the joy he finds in his long-term relationship with his companion, Janice; the harmony and beauty he finds in the natural world; and the deep bond of love that is re-established with his father and, later, with his son.

After his reconciliation with his son and following a visit to his son's home, he receives a letter:

> It means so much to me that we were able to spend that time with you. Your energy remains ever present in our home and in our hearts. Thanks for being my Pops, my father, and my friend. . . . Look at the moon tonight and think of us, and I will be looking at it and thinking of you.

The book is also enriched with Wilbur's reflections as a life-long college professor of psychology and practicing psychotherapist. Here again, one encounters a man who does not hide behind his professional role, but relates to his students and clients personally and directly. He reflects on both the joy found in bringing such a human element into his professional life and its cost.

But my words can only whet your appetite for the real thing. Let me make a closing comment on this remarkable book. At one point, Wilbur refers to the deeply insightful children's book, *The Velveteen Rabbit*. He includes a quotation from this book to illustrate his own view of what it means to lead a real life. In the story, the Skin Horse is replying to the Rabbit's question of how he became Real and says it is the result of his having been Really loved.

"Generally, by the time you are Real, most of your hair has been loved off, and your eyes drop out and you get loose in the joints and very shabby. But these things don't matter at all, because once you are Real you can't be ugly, except to people who don't understand."

What you will encounter in this book is a real human being, who has willingly paid the price of living life to its fullest, to opening his heart to genuine love, given and returned.

David Barstow

Preface

Standing at the railing of the walking bridge, looking into the Shetucket River below, I sense that people, their lives and relationships, are like rivers. Our branching streams touching the banks of others', their tributaries caressing our shores, one river flowing into and mingling with another, sweeping us away in the currents of our connecting lives. Like rivers, our merging and joining with others may be calming, cleansing, and healing, but it also may be raging or toxic, powerfully overwhelming. Some rivers nurture us, sustain us, replenish us through their strength, potency, and resilience—filled with the substance of life in their uncharted depths. Others are encumbered with snares, snarls, dangerous hazards that wound, bending swiftly in unexpected, unpredictable, and uncontrollable directions; still others are dammed, controlled, or polluted with poisons—drying up, dying. Even dried riverbeds, canyons, or gorges, created by once purposeful rivers long since ended and gone, remind and tell us of the life that was once there.

It should not surprise me that I see rivers in this way, because so much of our being—and our world—comprises water, because our religions, mythologies, and spiritual beliefs have long depicted life with the imagery of water and rivers. My Native American elders have believed for centuries that everything in life is connected; they use simple notions and basic elements to represent the source of our attachments, water being one of the most essential components. Native Americans also believe that life—symbolized by water—is cyclical, the ending of one life conjoining with, streaming into, the beginning of the next. Viewed in this way, all of our experiences are connected: our feelings and thoughts, our pains and wounds, our desires and dreams, our passions and human spirits. As revealed in the title essay, "Rivers of a Wounded Heart," and in the others included in this collection, all of our lives are anchored in these common waters—our home water—even though the specifics that define us as individuals may differ. Respect me, show caring for me, listen to me, speak with me honestly, directly, and I feel the same acceptance, covenance, and warmth in my heart as you feel in yours. Cut me and I feel the pain and bleed just as you do, no matter how the injury occurred or who inflicted it.

In my work as a psychotherapist and educator, I encounter so many wounded hearts—disconnected from feelings, disconnected from relationships with others, disconnected from life itself. Some are so still and silent as to appear lifeless, stagnant ponds with no inkling of stirring, disjoined from any linkage that may engage their emotions; others are so fierce, agitated, or furious that their mere appearance warns and cautions against our approach. Still others are so fragile that their balance may be altered by the smallest of perturbations. Merely stepping into the river, or skipping a stone across its surface, may change its essence. All relationships—between parents and siblings, partners and lovers, friends and colleagues, teachers and students—inevitably hurt us, wound us; no matter that they may also nourish and renew. People, like rivers, are life-taking as well as life-giving forces.

As a psychotherapist, I am someone who chooses to commerce with the forceful rivers of others' lives, akin to a deft river pilot. I guide people through the entangled mazes, the turbulent rushes of relationships, find the bridges that connect, seek the canals, the waterways, that free them from their constraining embankments, ultimately provide them with the faith to navigate, without my guidance, unfamiliar or frightening waters, and help them fathom the courage to heal hearts injured by the treacherous rivers they have already traveled.

I have learned to mend wounded hearts through the blending of two cultures—the Anishinabe (Chippewa or Ojibwa) heritage of my father, along with my acculturation to white society—and through the mutual enhancement of my relationships with others as a psychotherapist. It is the means to this reciprocal enrichment, the gift of these communal connections, that is shared in *Rivers of a Wounded Heart*. In the absence of real, honest, caring attachments to others, we will remain forever afflicted; the rivers of our lives will endure as meandering ribbons of toxins with neither the ability to nurture life nor to heal, with the capacity only to further desecrate, to impose and suffer additional pain—to damage more hearts. Even though poisonous imbalance or white water occurs in most rapids, if we seek the courage, the heart to traverse them, if we stay open to the reviving energy of the rivers that crisscross our lives, if we follow the currents of those who have negotiated pathways similar to ours, those who reveal to us the learning of their journeys, then the balance and calm will return, then our broken hearts may be eased—our dreams, our passions, our spirits restored.

Acknowledgements

Some of the stories in this book originally appeared in the publications listed below. My grateful acknowledgement is given to Monique Savlin, Ph.D., Editor of *Voices* (the journal of the American Academy of Psychotherapists) and to Dr. David Barstow, publisher and editor of *Pilgrimage* (Pilgrimage Press, Inc., 135 Sequoyah Ridge Road, Highlands, North Carolina 28741).

Wilbur, M. 2000. Pine island. *Pilgrimage 26*: 105–13.

Wilbur, M. 1999. Barn's burnt down . . . Now I can see the moon. *Voices 35* (1): 53–60.

Wilbur, M. 1999. Finding balance in the winds. *Journal for Specialists in Group Work 24* (4): 342–53.

Wilbur, M. 1999. Oz never gave to the tin man. *Voices 35* (3): 62–70.

Wilbur, M. 1999. The art of failing as a therapist. *Voices 35* (2): 31–39.

Wilbur, M. 1999. The rivers of a wounded heart. *Journal of Counseling and Development, Special Issue on Racism 77* (1) (Winter): 47–53.

Wilbur, M. 1998. Racehorse in the barn. *Voices 34* (Spring): 33–40.

Wilbur, M. 1998. The Vietnam attachment. *Voices 34* (4): 52–58.

Wilbur, M. 1998. Wizards, dragons, and 'prentices. *Voices 34* (2) (Summer): 60–66.

Wilbur, M. 1997. Cat's in the cradle/Little boy blue/Man in the moon. *Voices 33* (Winter): 55–63.

Wilbur, M. 1997. Day storms and night dreams. *Voices 33* (Summer): 77–85.

Wilbur, M. 1997. Storytelling: A therapist's guide to terminations. *Voices 33* (Fall): 63–70.

Wilbur, M. 1994. Groups and the velveteen rabbit: Process group effectiveness. *Voices 30* (Winter): 22–27.

Wilbur, M. 1994. Mavericks, renegades, and other cowboy therapists. *Voices 30* (Spring): 7–12.

Wilbur, M. 1993. In search of an honest voice. *Voices 29* (Winter): 84–88.

I also wish to acknowledge Dr. Janice Roberts Wilbur, my wife, partner, and colleague for twenty-six years, whose idea it was to submit the essays contained in *Rivers of a Wounded Heart* for publication in book form. She has been on the journey with me for all these years and, without her in my life, I would not have taken the risk to write on paper these deeply felt and personal aspects of my life.

With Janice's encouragement, I sent the manuscript to the Linda Chester Literary Agency in New York City and was contacted by Meredith Phelan, a literary agent for Linda Chester and Associates. Like Janice, Meredith has been and is one of the strongest advocates and supporters of my writing. Although I have expressed my appreciation to the Linda Chester Agency and Meredith many, many times, it is important to me that I recognize Meredith here for her significant and undaunted personal and professional assistance and consistency in finding a home for *Rivers of a Wounded Heart*. I am indeed fortunate for the serendipitous connection between Meredith and me and for her belief in me and my writing.

I likewise want to thank and express my appreciation to Capital Books, Inc., Noemi C. Taylor (editor), and Kathleen P.

Hughes (publisher) for their personal regard of me as a writer and for bringing *Rivers of a Wounded Heart* to a wider audience. I could not have found a better match between me and my writing and the people of Capital Books.

I would be remiss if I did not acknowledge two other people who have been instrumental in the development and publication of this book: Monique Savlin, editor of *Voices* (and the journal's board of editors and reviewers), and David Barstow, editor and publisher of *Pilgrimage*. I first began writing for *Voices* during Monique's editorship in 1994. Over the past eight years she has provided me with invaluable advice, criticism, and suggestions for my writing, and she has been a continuous source of encouragement and validation. Although I have been writing for David's publication for only a couple of years, he, too, has been a wonderful and greatly appreciated personal and professional source of confirmation and inspiration.

Many others have contributed to my life experiences and journey, not least of whom are the many, many students, professional colleagues, and clients I have encountered over the past twenty-six years. Some of these people are primary in my writing, while others remain in the background of my thoughts and feelings rather than appearing on paper, but they are no less significant in their contributions to *Rivers of a Wounded Heart.*

Finally, there are my friends and family whom I wish to acknowledge and recognize. I am the type of person who does not have a large number of friends, but I am truly blessed with the friends who are part of my life. James L. Frank is a sixty-three-year-old, curly-haired, eccentric, Italian guy with two Ph.D.s, one in mathematics and one in psychology, and two sailboats, one in Connecticut and one in

Florida, whom I met fifteen years ago in an airport in Great Britain while we were on our way to teach in Europe for Boston University (B.U.). Jim now lives only a few blocks from me in Connecticut, so we see each other often. During the last fifteen years, he has been through the good and bad times with me, always a loyal friend and confidant whom I cherish and love. Edil Torres Rivera I met, also in Europe—Germany—a few months after meeting Jim. Edil was in the army at the time and one of my students when I taught for B.U. After spending three years in Europe, I returned to the United States and a teaching position at the University of Connecticut. Shortly thereafter, Edil was transferred from Europe to West Point and once again became a student under my tutelage in his Ph.D. program. Edil calls me his mentor—which is only one aspect of our relationship—but, like Jim, Edil is a trusted, loyal, loving, and always consistent friend who is there for me should I need him, and when I don't. Then there is Michael Tlanusta (Walking Stick) Garrett whom I met only a few years ago. Michael is both friend and family. He is of mixed blood—Cherokee and Irish—and lives in North Carolina. He asked me if I would be his uncle, which is a very honorable and respectful request in Cherokee tradition. So I became Michael's uncle and he became my nephew—family. In addition, though, Michael is one of my most valued friends. His youthful, Cherokee wisdom gives me much strength and insight. Although geographical distance prevents us from seeing one another as often as we would like, Michael and I communicate often and he is a significant part of my life.

I have already mentioned Janice, but it is important that I acknowledge her on a more personal level as well. She said to me recently that she could not imagine what her life would be like without me in it, that I was her best friend, and that she has never been loved by anyone the way I have loved her. Sitting in our dimly lit living room when she said this to me, I had tears in my eyes and on my cheeks, but I merely listened rather than responding to her at the time. The context of our conversation is important, but I will not go into it here. Suffice it to say that she verbalized my feelings toward her in the words she said to me that evening. I usually think it is trite to use words like soul mate when describing a relationship with someone. But, in this instance and in my relationship with Janice, soul mate is the best I can do. Over the past twenty-six years, she has touched—and continues to touch—my heart, my soul, my mind, and my feelings as no other person has ever done. She is the most unselfish, giving, compassionate, caring, forthright, honest, perceptive, and loving person I have ever met, and I am so very, very fortunate and blessed to have shared so much of my life with her as my wife, partner, colleague, and best friend.

When Janice and I met, I had one son (Ross) and she had three children, one son (Jonathan) and two daughters (Christine and Catherine), by previous marriages. As all four have grown older, my relationships with them have changed from parent-child to adult-adult. Jon is now thirty-seven years old, Chris is thirty-five, Cathy is thirty-three, and Ross is thirty. There have been times with all of them—thankfully never at the same time—that our relationship was tumultuous and stormy. It is through these tough times that our relationships have become stronger and more intimate. Even though they are spread across the country geographically—Jon in Seattle, Chris in Wyoming, Cathy in Texas, and Ross in Colorado—I talk with them often and see them frequently. My relationship with each of them is very different; we talk about different things together, and their individual personalities, careers, and lifestyles are different. Nonetheless, each of them gives to me love and caring, for which I am very grateful and blessed to have in my life.

There are obviously others who have touched my life over the years who have not been mentioned here, but those I have acknowledged remain a constant source of friendship, strength, and love on my journey.

Chapter 1

Rivers of a Wounded Heart

> *We see some rivers better than we see others. For whatever reason—our histories with them . . .—a few such rivers (perhaps only one) come into focus for each of us more readily and significantly than the rest. They grow into places of deep fixity in life and align themselves like compass points in the mind's geography. . . . When times come, as they invariably do, when what is needed most is a form of existential triage, I am certain that if I can just get back to this place, equilibrium will somehow return. . . . I don't know whether this means that my [river] is a starting point or an ending point. Perhaps just a point of vantage. But I think this feeling, more than anything, is what is meant . . . [by]"home water."*
>
> — Leeson, *The Unspecifiable Eloquence of Rivers*

My brother and I stood on the corner in front of Vic and Billie's, the local prescription drug store and teenage soda-fountain hangout. It was a warm summer evening in the mid-1950s. Although my brother was seven years my senior, and I was almost nine, it was atypical for me to accompany him "downtown."

As we stood with a group of other boys judging which cars "tooling" Main Street were the coolest, two of my brother's friends arrived at the corner and walked up to us. One asked, "Who's the little spic kid?" I knew the pejorative meaning of "spic," because the small Michigan mill town of my boyhood was a hub for Mexican migrant workers every summer—working the mint, onion, and cucumber fields of the rich, muck soil—and the locals were anything but kind in their racist, wounding comments and derisive attitudes.

I had never been referred to as "spic," although my complexion was especially dark that summer from spending hours in the Midwest sun playing sandlot baseball. Even normally, it was very different from that of my brother and sister, who were fair-skinned and freckle-faced and had auburn hair. My hair was "jet black," as my mother described it.

My brother responded to his friend's comment, "Careful, he'll pull his blade. He's my kid brother."

"Different father?"

"No, same father."

"Mother then?"

"No, same mother." I was too intimidated and young to engage the older boys in stinging adolescent banter, so I said nothing, and they eventually went on to other conversations about girls, cars, and sports. As the crowd on the corner of Vic and Billie's grew larger, I told my brother it was getting late and I had better leave.

Walking the six blocks home, I crossed the bridge over the river that surrounded our small island town, stopping midway to watch the woolen mill's old waterwheel revolve slowly in the river's current, thoughts spinning in my head and my heart filled with feelings. As I stood on the bridge, watching the river and its waterwheel, I thought about the trip my family had taken from Michigan to the Wisconsin town of Oneida three years earlier.

En route to the farmhouse where my father had lived with his biological father, mother, three brothers, and sister, we stopped at a small tourist attraction, a "trading post" just outside Oneida, and my father bought me a cheap Indian headdress for children and a rubber mallet tomahawk. It was a hot day, so we also stopped on the banks of the Wisconsin River to go wading. Because the river water was cold, I waded for only a few minutes. As I climbed the bank of the river from the cold water, my sister, who was nine years older, began to scream. I had leeches, "blood suckers," my brother called them, covering both legs from ankle to thigh. One look and I, too, began to scream. My father lovingly scooped me into his arms, sat down on the riverbank with me in his lap, and carefully held a lighted match over each of the parasites adhered to my skin, causing them to curl and drop from my legs.

My father was born in the old farmhouse, close to the Lac du Flambeau Indian Reservation, shortly after his father and mother had moved there from Hennepin County, Minnesota, in 1915. All we found of the house that day was its crumbling foundation, overgrown in the midst of acres of empty fields. As the story goes, told in bits and pieces during our trip to Oneida, my father's father had been killed in a fight on the nearby reservation when my father was in his early teens. Shortly thereafter, my father's brother, Mike, who was the eldest son and after whom I was named, committed suicide in a cornfield near the old farmhouse; my father was enlisted by his mother in the Civilian Conservation Corps, and he was sent to northern Minnesota—Gooseberry Falls—to help build a stone bridge over the Gooseberry River.

After three years with the Civilian Conservation Corps, my father returned to the farmhouse in Wisconsin to discover that his mother had remarried and moved to Michigan. He followed his family there, found them, changed his last name to that of his stepfather, and began working as an automobile mechanic. A few years later he met my mother—whose last name, surprisingly, was the same as that of his stepfather's and his own new last name—and they were married. He and my mother never left the small mill town on the Grand River where they met, and I grew up, the son of a "drunken Indian"—no less or more pejorative than "spic."

Although I do recall positive aspects of my childhood experiences and memories, many of these early images and recollections were a prelude to more occurrences (too numerous to mention here) of racism, bigotry, prejudice, and exclusion that would affect me. The important influence of these early images and incidents, however, was that I "took the challenge," as my father encouraged me to do. Sadly, he was of another time and generation (a "half-breed" Chippewa) and succumbed to the Native American stereotypes of alcohol abuse and unemployment, despite his efforts (I realized as an adult) to assimilate, acculturate, and live the Norman Rockwell vision of the American melting pot. For me, the river—with its old woolen mill, waterwheel, and bridge—would become a place where I found insight and made decisions.

The mill itself was located on the banks of the Grand River, at the intersection of Michigan Highways 50 and 99

(M50 and M99), which, with the bridge over the river, established the northern boundary of the small island city. To the south of the small town, the Grand River forked to the east and west and rejoined at the river's north bridge, forming a natural island that had once been a center for gristmills and mineral baths.

When I was a boy, my route to school took me daily to the intersection of M50 and M99. At this intersection, the sidewalk widened as it passed the front entrance of the woolen mill, crossed the north bridge of the river, and led to the downtown stores and shops. At the south end of town, the sidewalk narrowed to a small walking bridge that took me over the river again to the elementary and high schools, located on the river's south bank.

My mother, who worked the looms of the woolen mill, feared the river. Each morning, from a third-floor window of the mill, she watched for me on my way to school as I intersected M50 and M99, passed the front entrance to the mill, and traversed the north bridge of the river. Daily, I would stop on the bridge and stare, fascinated, at the mill's old waterwheel, still turned by the river. Although I didn't fear the river, I respected my mother's warnings. Little did I know she was always watching, worried, from her third-floor window, as I stood momentarily to gaze at the river and the old waterwheel.

When the mill closed in the spring of 1957, my mother began a job at the pickle factory, a cannery that had recently relocated from Wisconsin. She worked for the next twenty-five years as a manual laborer on the cannery's conveyor belts, inserting processed cucumbers (pickles) into glass jars, by hand, as they passed in front of her on the conveyor belt.

In the fall of 1957, as I approached the abandoned woolen mill on my way to school, I stopped at the intersection of M50 and M99. As I looked at the soundless building, no longer clanging and scraping with the friction of the whirring monster machines inside, I was flooded with an awareness of my first eleven years of life. The father I knew was someone different from the father my brother and sister had known; at least that's what they told me. They were two and four, respectively, when he went to war; returning from the 101st Airborne Division, D-Day, Normandy, Bastogne, Paris, and Berlin four years later, in 1945. I was a post-World War II baby (a baby boomer); my sister and brother said my Dad was a drunk and that I looked like him. All I knew and believed until this point was that my Dad was a war hero who had received two Silver Stars for bravery in battle, and his army buddies called him "Chief." Very impressive stuff, in 1957, for an eleven-year-old boy.

My earlier images of racism and bigotry merged with new understanding and reality as I stood at the intersection that fall day. My sister had become pregnant out-of-wedlock and left home three years earlier, before graduating from high school. My brother's girlfriend also had become pregnant during the summer of '57, and he, too, had left home without finishing high school. Mom had just begun her new job at the cannery, Dad was drinking heavily, and the home front was more conflict-ridden and combative than usual. Dad hadn't worked in some time, although he had tried assembly lines at several factories. He was now working sporadically as a plumber's helper.

I looked across the north bridge, where M50 and M99 merged and led to points south and east. To my right, M50 curved in a westerly direction. Behind me, M99 followed a true north course. My turning point that day was literal as well as cerebral and emotional. I turned slowly, clockwise, in my Converse high-tops: first, facing toward M50 and the west; then turning north toward M99; and, finally, returning to my original direction facing where M50 and M99 merged and crossed the north bridge. I then reversed direction and rotated counterclockwise to examine the intersection and its directions once more.

At the tender and naive age of eleven, I made a decision and pledge to myself: I would find a new life for myself—different from that of my parents and siblings. My route to this new and different life would involve two of my strongest resources, academics and athletics. I could not live my life in a small island town, working a menial job in a mill, cannery, or automotive factory. Some day I would leave my home water for a different, better life.

Obviously, there were many other events, some of them tragic, that I have omitted involving racism, a poverty-level family, and alcohol abuse. But it was the pledge I made near the river of my boyhood, and my newfound insight, standing in front of the abandoned and silenced woolen mill, that provided the critical momentum for the next forty years of my life.

My professional development and decisions (most, typically, unpredicted) have always included working with, counseling, and teaching students of color (Native Americans, African Americans, Latinos), who have, in turn, influenced my counseling and teaching. My approach has evolved into and is based on a perspective of circularity and nonlinearity, with ordered patterns emerging from the disorder of chaos.

Professionally, I have come to believe that human beings' theoretical ways of making meaning in the world are constructions—stories we tell to make sense of what we experience as a result of life's particularly critical incidents. How people perceive, interpret, and recount past events are surely as important as the events themselves. They show how people make sense of their experiences and use them to cope with the present and make decisions about the future. They explain how people develop over time and allow an analysis of subjective experience in response to specific events and incidents.

I have also found such experiences to be more complicated and less predetermined than can be explained by theories that focus on processes that reproduce psychological capacities, stages, and proclivities across generations. Rarely is there a fixed consequence of any single event. Unfortunately, traditional models of therapy often are based on linear assumptions of causality, so they focus their treatment efforts on the apparent linear development and causes of the client's life-events and problems. Practitioners should be aware that the experiences and life-events that clients describe, by their very nature, are focused initially on a narrow time frame and seem linear. It is only with attention to longer time frames that different, nonlinear perspectives may overcome the client's, and the therapist's, view of linear causality.

For example, I could have chosen to follow the life pattern of my parents and siblings, or developed a drinking problem based on the predisposition of my father, rather than choosing the course I did follow. Instead, I left my home water in 1965, taking M50 and M99 southwest, to attend Western Michigan University on an academic scholarship. Since that time, I survived the Vietnam War; completed a doctorate in counseling psychology; and lived, worked with, counseled, and taught people of color in most regions of the continental United States and overseas.

However, with the completion of my doctorate in 1975, and the decision to become an academician and teacher of therapists, came a fifteen-year life as an "academic nomad"—with frequent geographic moves—similar to the itinerant lifestyle of many Native Americans. Each new place continued the Native American bequest, reflecting the legacy of Native American influence in the names of their tribes, places, and rivers: Ohio's Miamis and the Cuyahoga River; Cedar Falls and the Iowas' (Ioways') Blackhawk River; the Chippewa (Ojibwa), Fond du Lac Indian Reservation, and Whiteface River of northern Minnesota; the Cherokee Nation of Oklahoma and the Arkansas River; the Onondagas of Syracuse; Philadelphia's Schuylkill River and the Delaware (Lenni Lenape) of Pennsylvania; the Nez Perces and Appaloosa horses of Washington State and the Palouse (Palus) of Pullman; the Shetucket and Willimantic Rivers, and the Mashantucket, Pequot, and Mohegan tribes of Connecticut.

The Ojibwa, with whom I worked and taught for more than four years, gave me a hand-beaded medallion when I left Minnesota for a position in Oklahoma. The rose flower depicted on the pendant represented life's circle. Our paths would cross again in the repeating circle of life. A few months later, when my partner and wife (Janice) also left Minnesota for Syracuse University, the Chippewa honored her with a "dance around the drum" (a circle) and a golden eagle feather to guide and protect her in her continued life journey—two of the Ojibwas' most sacred honors and traditions.

Although there are many ways to define one's ethnicity and cultural identity (biologically, socially, culturally, or by self-identity), I realized, through the contrast of these two farewell experiences with the Ojibwa, that I had followed vestiges of my father's time and generation—toward acculturation and assimilation. Janice was recognized by the Chippewa as a member of their tribe, whereas I was acknowledged for how I had socialized and defined myself: "marginal," that is, conflicted, unable to form dual ethnic identity, only marginally familiar with the norms of either Native American or white culture.

For as long as I can remember, I have been at the margin of dominant American culture, much longer than I have sometimes been willing to admit or accept. I also realize I play a part in my "marginalization," through both my unwillingness to compromise that which I truly believe with dominant American values, and my appearance. Three years ago, I found the courage to grow my hair long enough for a ponytail, and I recently retrieved my boots and Levi's from the closet—still marginalized. But my marginalization is due mostly to the passion of my beliefs that a wounded heart continues to be inflicted with injury by assaults from the collective commonality of those who cannot, or will not, tolerate difference. Those who are literal, linear, and cause-effect thinkers; those who harbor, yet deny, their bigotry and prejudice; those for whom their perception alone is "reality"; and those who, knowingly and unknowingly, maintain and perpetuate the "isms" within my country have wounded my heart, and the hearts of others, with their raging rivers of racism.

Nevertheless, I have found solace, and helped my students and clients to find comfort, in everyday experiences and natural phenomena that behave chaotically, nonlinearly, differently, and with great complexity: transforming clouds before a storm; sunrises and sunsets; flowers, plants, trees; waterfalls; the clamor of city traffic; smoke rising from a chimney; snowflakes; and, most of all, rivers. All are experiences and incidents of life—and people—that cannot be predetermined, predicted, or controlled.

Seven years ago, Janice and I purchased a stately Victorian home near the Willimantic River and the intersection of Connecticut Highways 32 and 66; the old, abandoned, and silenced American Thread Mill is there, with a walking bridge over the river. Considering the river and junction at which my journey began, its bends and nonlinear curves have led me in a wide and circular path to a very privileged position in life. And, although the waterwheel of the old American Thread Mill is long since gone, the river is home water nonetheless—though the wounded heart will never mend. For, as a former student and now beloved friend and colleague Edil Torres Rivera once taught me, *"No se puede tapar el cielo con la mano"* (You cannot cover the sky with your hand), something a Native American might very well say.

Chapter 2

In Search of an Honest Voice

In 1966, while he was at the Merrill Palmer Institute in Detroit, Clarke Moustakas wrote an unpublished monograph entitled "Honesty, Idiocy, and Manipulation." I didn't read the Moustakas monograph, however, until 1977, after completing my formal education in counseling. I began my career in counseling at a young age; I received my B.S. in behavioral and experimental psychology in 1968 (at the age of twenty-one), my M.A. in counseling at age twenty-two (in 1969) and my Ed.D. in counselor education and counseling psychology in 1975 (at twenty-eight)—including a four-year interruption for military service during the Vietnam War. Since 1969, I have been a drug counselor for Vietnam combat veterans, a high school teacher, the director of a college counseling center, and a professor of counseling psychology at seven different universities—counting three years in Germany teaching in an Overseas Counseling Program.

After twenty-six years in the counseling profession, I find myself returning to this one obscure piece of literature: "Honesty, Idiocy, and Manipulation." This may be due, in part, to the lack of specialization of my research agenda and my practice and teaching of counseling and therapy. Or just as likely, it may be due to my insistent adherence to the more holistic perspective of a generalist.

In any event, I have researched and published in a number of professional journals, an array of research results and topics related to counseling and therapy—despite my generalist attitude and lack of focused specialization. I also have remained reasonably familiar with the expanding literature, research, and professional journals concerned with counseling and the therapeutic process, and have managed to keep abreast of the increasingly complex (and seemingly "magical") statistical procedures used by researchers to quantify research results and to objectify the process of therapy.

Ironically, given my erratic career path, I coordinated a counseling psychology program at a major land-grant university for five years and received tenure in 1992, for the first time. Intertwined with these professional activities, and more important I believe, have been significant and very personal events, people, relationships, and developmental tasks.

First among these is the Vietnam War and the impact it had, and still has, on my life. The second is "the divorce," and my sixteen-year struggle to maintain, nurture, and develop the meaningful relationship I now have with my son, Ross. The third, and perhaps most important, aspect of my personal development is my marriage to and twenty-six-year relationship with my current partner, Janice. In addition to the normal support and conflict of any intimate relationship, we have both struggled personally and professionally to maintain the quality of that relationship, and to enhance each other's development. Even though she and I both have doctorates in counseling, this struggle has often been compounded and exacerbated by our own, as well as societal and institutional, gender-role conflicts and stereotypes, the blending of children from earlier marriages into a new family, and maintaining and developing two careers.

This cursory listing of developmental issues has omitted some earlier, yet important and major, people and developmental events and tasks that have influenced who I am as a person. Not least among them is growing up in a poverty-level, lower socioeconomic family and neighborhood, a World War II "hero-father" with a drinking problem, a mother who worked as a laborer her entire life, two older siblings who dropped out of high school in the tenth grade, and my being a first-generation college student supported by academic and athletic scholarships.

However, I'd like to focus on another developmental issue and perspective. I believe that the most direct and effective way to enhance and integrate human development, whether it is our own or others', is by being honest with ourselves and relating honestly to others. This seems like such a simple task, yet, sadly, I find few among us who can be honest about who they are and speak honestly to others. Likewise, I have found few who genuinely want to listen to others speak honestly about themselves and their developmental issues. Also sadly, I have not found many of my colleagues to be supportive of enhancing and developing this. I can count on one hand those I have found.

Many in my profession are more concerned about professionalism than development. They appear more concerned with political correctness than moral rightness, more concerned with their own individual advancement than the enhancement of others' development, and more concerned with quantitative and objective methods of studying people than qualitative and subjective ways of understanding and relating to them. I am certain that many of my more objective and professional colleagues think my hair is still too long, my mustache too bushy, my dress too casual, my language too secular and earthy—profane —and my personal honesty and disclosure too disarming to meet their criteria for professionalism.

Despite all this, however, I continue to return to this obscure 1966 monograph by Clarke Moustakas: "Honesty, Idiocy, and Manipulation." Moustakas, more than others I have read, captures the essence of honesty and the synonymous terms of authenticity, genuineness, and congruence.

> I am honest when what I communicate is consistent with my real feelings, even when these depart sharply from the perceptions of others. . . . The integrating meaning in perception determines the nature of individual reality, not the number of objects or traits tabulated by a machine or observed in a detached manner. . . . Honesty refers to the self of the person, the person's own search for truth. My task in honesty is to maintain an allegiance to my own self. (Moustakas 1977, 59, 60)

Could it be this simple: being honest with oneself and others? Why have we counselors and therapists abandoned our attention to honesty, authenticity, congruence, and genuineness: because such concepts are not easily measured and quantified? Or is the reason more primal: Have most people, including professional therapists, deviated from the truth in the form of lies, evasion, self-denial, and distortion motivated by a wish to influence, change, direct, control, or have power over others? Are dishonesty and distortion motivated by fear, as a way of manipulating other people by preventing them from discovering their real thoughts and feelings? Is dishonesty an attempt to provide the illusion of self-control and protection of one's own life? Is the lie the instrument used to avoid the difficulties, pain, and conflict we all experience? Or is dishonesty the crux of the difficulty, pain, and conflict most people experience in their lives and their relationships with others?

Realizing these are not popular questions to ponder in an era of "why ask why," "just do it" political correctness, and litigious solutions to human conditions, it is time to return to these basic questions and concepts in therapy and in our own lives, despite societal constraints, norms, and expectations to the contrary.

As to my own answers and conclusions, after twenty-six years of counseling, teaching, researching, and scholarly reading, I find few among us who have the courage to risk being honest with themselves and others. More frequently, I find myself interacting with socially and professionally contrived roles. Rarely do I find simple, open, direct honesty and authenticity through self-disclosure, feedback, and practical confrontation.

Too often, I have encountered professional counselors and therapists who were more concerned with advancing and promoting their own career and political agenda (via professionally correct and appropriate behaviors, words, and roles) than expressing themselves directly, honestly, and personally. Too often, I have encountered counselors who treated my personal, developmental issues—a young lower-class school boy's attempt to overcome the odds against his success, Vietnam, divorce, gender-role conflicts, difference in socioeconomic background—with detached objectivity, statistically valid and reliable assessment instruments, and the jargon, labels, and nomenclature of their profession, rather than responding to me honestly, personally, and with ordinary human caring. And, too often, I encounter student-counselors who seek only the cookbook content and technically correct neatness necessary to attain the required credit hours, degree, and credentials leading to professional certification or licensure and the industry of third-party payments, rather than enhancing and integrating their own personal development, individual attributes, and human ability to relate personally and honestly to others.

Nor do I believe we will find the questions or answers to the problems of humankind through quantitative methods and statistical procedures alone. Similarly, I do not believe the questions and answers will be found in development and implementation of further rules, laws, techniques, or ethical standards and guidelines to define and govern our professional—and social—behavior and relationships.

Rather, the questions we must ask ourselves, personally and professionally, are why we have abandoned honesty with ourselves and others in favor of dishonesty manifested through the enactment of socially and professionally appropriate (and politically correct) words, behaviors, and roles. Our professional agenda and roles may have been set by Freud himself, in his own denial of reality and truth through his abandonment of the seduction theory. Or, as Moustakas so simply puts it,

> Rarely is honesty the best policy from the standpoint of freedom from suffering or achievement of material gain. In a competitive society, the honest person is considered naive, immature, and child-like. . . . The honest person, trying to live simply, directly and openly is often regarded with suspicion and imputed with evil and hidden motives. (Moustakas 1977, 60, 61)

> The honest person is supported and valued at times, by some individuals, but almost inevitably at some point, at least in our present society, the simple man is doubted and his motives questioned. (Moustakas 1966, 3)

So, it is time for me to stop hiding under the porch and licking the wounds of my developmental tasks. It is time, for me and others, to reinvest in the need and capacity to speak personally and honestly about ourselves and who we are, to support and enhance others' ability to speak personally and honestly about themselves and their development, and to provide more ears and voices that advocate the honest aspects of our profession. It is time to provide a more equal balance to the profession's current overemphasis on professional activities; individual advancement; professionally and politically correct behaviors, skills, and roles; and the espoused effectiveness and objectivity of quantitative procedures, alone, to address individuals' developmental issues and their integration.

There is as great a need today as there was in 1966 for counselors and therapists who are willing to listen to those who need and are also willing to express themselves directly and honestly, in a way that is consistent with their own personal experience and development.

This simplistic answer is not to be perceived merely as lamenting for times past or the good old days of personal introspection, awareness, and discovery, although these most certainly are avenues leading to honesty. "If the one who lies is the same as the one to whom the lie is told, then he must know, in his capacity as deceiver, the truth which is hidden from him as the one deceived" (Shlien 1960, 297). "Experience has convinced me . . . that the patient does not 'invent' but always tells the truth, even though in a distorted form" (Masson 1992, 165). And, although Einstein (at age twenty-two) may have been correct, "If Diogenes were alive today, he'd be looking in vain for an honest person with his lantern" (*The Chronicle of Higher Education* 1992, B5), I am still hopeful.

I have decided, as did Moustakas, on a parsimonious answer and a seemingly neglected, if not abandoned, principle and concept that is central to our own personal well-being, our clients' well-being, our professional research and educational agenda, and our professional and social effectiveness: honesty.

I have a faded, underlined, dog-eared copy of the 1966 Moustakas monograph, still reproducible, in case you have difficulty finding it in your personal library.

Chapter 3

Storytelling: A Therapist's Guide to Terminations

This writing represents the progression of my thoughts and learning about terminations and endings, of therapeutic relationships and others, since my first attempt to understand them in a group communication class over twenty-five years ago. Our class assignment: write a paper that would address termination (saying goodbye) as a significant component of our learning process. I hadn't a clue and I failed the task miserably! Although I could not complete the lesson successfully, what I did learn was that I had avoided all the significant endings of my life so far.

In the intervening years, I have come to believe that saying goodbye is one of life's most fundamental tasks. It is an individual's life-story, a humanistic and existential aspect of ourselves, involving our feelings of love for and caring about the loss of people, places, and events of our lives. At the same time, we experience fear, hurt, anger, and ambivalent feelings toward this same trilogy. As such, emotions are the essence of saying goodbye, and their meaning and disclosure are essential to the resolution of that which is ending: the events, places, and relationships that are grounded in the emotional experience of our lives. And, in our role as therapists, one of our most elemental roles may well be that of helping our clients to negotiate the emotional boundaries and landmarks of their lives' endings, losses, and terminations.

The way we make meaning in the world is through constructions—stories our clients tell to help us make sense of what they feel and experience. Their telling of such stories may enrich and change their (and our) old meanings and feelings and enable us to practice therapy with more relevance. At best, the telling of such stories assists our clients and ourselves to realize what goodbyes still need to be said and the benefit of having said goodbye to what has ended or changed.

As a corollary, and having been profoundly influenced by Sidney Jourard's seminal work in self-disclosure, I have similarly discovered my own storytelling to be a trenchant means of overcoming clients' blocks to self-disclosure at significant ending points in their lives.

My premise, of course, is that for therapists to guide clients through the topology of their life-story goodbyes, they must first traverse the configurations of their own life-journey's losses and terminations. After all, one becomes an expert guide by becoming familiar and comfortable with the territory being explored by others. Thus, through the storytelling disclosure of the losses and endings of our lives, we may better guide our clients in finding their way as well.

Over the past twenty years, I have told clients and students stories of my own significant losses and endings to overcome blocks to their storytelling, to guide them in resolving their difficult points of termination and loss, and to find a way to say goodbye to those relationships, places, and life-events that are changing or coming to an end. Obviously, my stories are not of equal emotional weight, but they are nonetheless important in their own right, because they focus on different kinds of losses—some that relate to life-events, some that represent significant places in my life, and others that describe my loss of people and relationships.

There were few goodbyes in my early life, growing up in a small mill town in Michigan; the death of thirteen-year-old "Scamp," my beagle dog, was my first significant loss. My father placed him in the passenger seat of his truck one summer morning, and said to me, "We're going for a ride." He returned a couple of hours later with alcohol on his breath. As he approached me, sitting on the step of the back porch, he tried to hide his .22 caliber pistol by slipping it into the back pocket of his overalls; I knew Scamp was never coming home again. The death of "Gramma Pearl," in my junior year of high school, was much more significant; but my experience and understanding of life and death were too naive to allow me to truly comprehend its meaning. She lived with our family for several years before moving to her own small apartment two years before she died. During those two years, I spent Saturday afternoons with her—taking her grocery shopping, eating a small lunch of Campbell's tomato soup and bologna sandwiches, and watching her crochet doilies and pillow slipcovers as she listened to the turmoil of my adolescence. I visited her in the hospital the night she died—after basketball practice. I left while she was still alive, listening to the rasping breaths of emphysema (thirty years working in the woolen mills) as I left her room. But, I never told her goodbye—I never told her how much I loved her, that her passing would leave an immense hole in my life.

I first began to seriously think about the meaning of saying goodbye while I was in the military, searching for and finding the dead bodies of Hurricane Camille's rubble in the back-bay waters of Biloxi, Mississippi. Still in the military, I again thought of the meaning of saying goodbye while counseling combat veterans with traumatic, brutal, and unsaid goodbyes to their fellow soldiers, friends, and companions in the jungles of Vietnam. Today, I still have unsaid goodbyes to these men and women who return to me from time to time in the darkness of night and restless sleep.

I thought about the meaning of saying goodbye some more when my six-week-old son was given a fifty-fifty chance of living and, if he did, with a high probability that he would be mentally retarded. That same year, more meaning was added when I was diagnosed inaccurately with a terminal illness and given a life expectancy of twelve to fifteen years. I discovered five years later that the diagnosis was incorrect, but, during the five-year interim, I began to make significant decisions based on these events. I began to say goodbye to what had ended in my life: a decision not to return to and live in the hometown of my boyhood and a decision to divorce.

Although both decisions were significant and involved losses and endings, there was little left, emotionally, to resolve with my wife or hometown. My marriage was long past the point of unhappiness and misery for us both, although the separation from my son would continue to be a source of painful conflict and guilt. The connection with my hometown, I realized, had ended when I left for college. I never returned home to live, only for an occasional visit, and the option of working in a factory of the automotive industry was not appealing to me.

What I did not realize, however, was that these endings would become the beginning of many more endings, losses, and terminations. With the decision to end my marriage came the decision to pursue a doctorate in counseling psychology, to which my wife had objected. And, with completion of my doctorate and my decision to become an academician and teacher of therapists came fifteen years as an "academic nomad," with frequent geographic moves and endings with significant places in my life.

My goodbye to Western Michigan University on completion of my final degree was especially arduous. A new stone wall was being constructed around the classroom building where I had spent five years learning to be a psychologist. I climbed one of the mounds of rocks surrounding the building in the late afternoon of my last day at the university, painstakingly choosing a few of the smaller rocks to take with me. As the sun set behind the maple trees' frost-tinged, red-orange leaves and the duck pond of the North Valley campus, tears were leaking from my eyes. One of my professors was leaving the building and, as he passed by my perch atop the rocks, he quipped, with his typical clinical objectivity and professional distance, "Separation anxiety's a bitch, isn't it?" When he was out of sight, the moistness of my eyes turned to rivers of tears and, to myself, I said goodbye to Western—stones tightly clasped in both hands.

I said goodbye to Hiram College with an extended middle finger defiantly thrust, from the driver's window of the U-Haul truck, into the snowy and empty night in January, heading west toward Iowa. I left the University of Northern Iowa—"A Place to Grow" aptly painted on the roadway sign dividing the Illinois and Iowa state lines—long before my students and I were ready for the termination, but the grant supporting my position had ended, with no possibility of renewal. At the same time, I said goodbye to one of my most significant mentors for the last time, in his hotel room at a Chicago conference. He died of leukemia a few months later.

Five years later, I said goodbye to the University of Minnesota, The Native American Indian Project, Duluth, Lake Superior, and the people with whom I had formed close and meaningful relationships—as the result of yet another expired grant that supported my position. Part of that goodbye found me sitting on a bench at the pier on Lake Superior's harbor, next to the aerial bridge, replaying "the talks" with my father while the two of us sat on that same bench almost a year before he died.

I left Minnesota in January, five months after the death of my father, for a position at the University of Tulsa. When the College of Education was dissolved three years later, which I learned by reading the Sunday morning headline of the *Tulsa World,* I said goodbye to the University of Tulsa and headed east to Philadelphia and a one-year position as a distinguished visiting scholar. Leaving Tulsa was one of the uglier, but most principled, of my goodbyes—too involved to detail here. Ironically, I sold some of my household furniture and items to raise enough money to rent the truck for the move east and move into an apartment once there.

The following year, I said yet another goodbye to the neighborhood of North Philadelphia and to Temple University—one of the best years of my life, professionally and personally. I moved to Pullman, Washington, and began a year of role-reversal as a house-husband, under the guise, of course, of being an academic and writer on sabbatical.

Secretly, this, too, was one of the best places of my life. After a year of golden wheat fields, unemployment, and the "Palouse" of Washington State, I said, *"auf Wiedersehen, Amerika,"* and escaped to West Berlin and a position with Boston University, to find a new place.

Although leaving important places in our lives involves significant loss, for me it is the ending and change in relationships with people that result in the weighty emotional riposte of our goodbye.

I said goodbye to my son, Ross, and experienced a change in my relationship with him, when his mother and I were divorced. She had gained custody after a long and, in hindsight, regretted custody battle. As a consequence of my not returning him from a visitation in a timely manner, I was not permitted to see him for three years. During this time, I realized the message and wisdom of King Solomon. I let go and said goodbye to what could no longer be, rather than continuing to tear my son apart.

I was with my father when he died on his living room floor, after spending eight hours, his last, saying goodbye to each other in the late darkness of night and gray twilight of morning. We took drags from the same cigarettes, held hands, sat silently together wrapped in each other's arms, reminisced about the good and bad times of his waning life and our time together, and said goodbye. Having missed the opportunity with Gramma Pearl, I told him while he was alive how much I loved him and that his passing was to leave a wound on my heart that would never heal. I said my final goodbye to him with a silent salute and the tears of my heart at his military funeral, holding the hand of my nine-year-old son standing by my side. I planted two mountain ash trees on each side of his headstone a year later, the last time I visited his grave. Because he was the eldest son, my brother received the American flag that draped his coffin, a part of my father's life and death I covet to this day.

Leaving Minnesota involved an agonizing goodbye to Janice as a result of my professional move to Oklahoma and hers to Syracuse University. Although we were reunited a year later when she joined the faculty of Tulsa University, I do not believe I have ever been as despondent and empty as the time we were apart. I will always recall the drive on southbound I-35 from Duluth to Tulsa, when I was unable to stem the flow of tears and the thought of her absence from my daily life.

Again, I was faced with saying goodbye to Janice when I left Washington State and went to Europe—at the risk of losing my relationship with her! She remained at Washington State University. We said our goodbyes in the driveway of our rented house, as we were leaving for the bus station and the imminent ride to the airfields of Spokane and Europe, holding each other in our arms while passersby gawked at our tears and implacable embrace. As we held each other, she whispered, "People are strong, Michael; relationships are fragile. But we have to risk losing them to keep them." I spent three years in Europe rekindling my passion for therapy and teaching, more than two of them with Janice after seducing her to join me in West Berlin. Shortly after the Berlin Wall came down, we both returned to Amerika and the University of Connecticut.

In our time together Janice has been the most significant and loved person in my personal and professional life. For more than twenty-six years, she has helped me take things "down off the shelf" when they are out of my reach.

After many years of separation, Ross and I also rekindled our relationship as father (Pops and, more recently, "Edutsi"—the Cherokee word for old man) and son. He attended the University of Connecticut for one academic year, but transferred to Western Michigan University (my alma mater). The goodbye we said on the day of his return to the Midwest was one of my most painful losses and endings. As he drove down the driveway and turned onto the first road that led him back to Michigan, I ran after his car to catch one last glimpse of him. The dust of the dry, dirt road engulfed his car and billowed into the early spring morning as the red of his taillights faded to nothingness. He didn't see my uplifted and wavering arm, trying despairingly to let go and hang on at the same time. Walking back to the house, I knelt and picked up a small stone from the gravel driveway. Tears welled in my eyes, the pain of that goodbye overwhelming me as I tried to keep breathing against the mountainous pressure deep in my chest. I wept, guttural sounds of grief emerging from the depths of my being, crouched on my knees in the driveway, gently rubbing the surface of the small stone as I said goodbye to the ten months we had living together as father and son. I still have the small stone from the gravel driveway safely stored in a drawer, knowing that we will never again live together as father and son.

My old professor was right; separation and loss make people feel anxious and fearful. Separation and termination involve a sense of loss and hurt and anger that something valuable is being taken away. Many people, including me, try to avoid the threat and pain of separation and termination.

We use such euphemisms as "so long," "see ya," "take care." We promise to write, phone, visit, or keep in touch. We may even plan a reunion, knowing all along that it will never happen, or at least that our relationship will never be the same. We may become so busy with other things that the goodbyes never get said. Or we may choose to remain in relationships, jobs, careers, and places long past the point of unhappiness and misery. The status quo, even when it is miserable, is at least familiar. Nevertheless, the awesome burden of trying to hang on to what is over and done makes us even more miserable.

Life inevitably involves a series of terminuses, and it is vitally important to acknowledge each post and stone along the way, from station to station, and to express our feelings as we pass each one. I have come to realize in the course of my own travel that those boundary markers are not in a linear line. Moreover, our lives and paths are not unrelated and discrete points and lines in time, but overlapping circles, the trajectories of their limits and boundaries oscillating and pulled toward divergent attractors, but circles nonetheless.

The Ojibwa with whom I worked and taught for more than four years in Minnesota gave me a hand-beaded medallion when we said goodbye. They told me the rose depicted on the pendant represented life's circle. They believed our paths would cross again: there were no endings, only a repeating circle of life. When Janice left Minnesota for Syracuse, the Chippewa honored her with a "dance around the drum" (a circle) and a golden eagle feather to guide and protect her in her life-journey—two of the Ojibwas' most sacred honors and traditions. Janice, and the Chippewa who danced with her around the drum, already knew what I was still learning about saying goodbye. The circle of my life continues to overlap, again and again, with Janice; with Ross, who is healthy, intelligent, twenty-five years old, and a high school teacher and soccer coach in northern Michigan; and with other significant people, places, and life-events that keep the circle alive.

A few years ago, Janice and I purchased an old Queen Ann Victorian house in Willimantic, Connecticut, an old mill town on the Willimantic River and an iteration of the circle that began on the mill town river of my boyhood. The circle of an earlier boyhood goodbye also came around, a year after we moved into the house, when I buried a loyal, eight-year companion—my buddy, "Soda Pop"—but with far more intensity than I had ever felt with the loss of a dog. I am certain my professional colleagues thought it trivial and mundane but, the day Soda Pop was euthanized I took off from work to bury him and say goodbye. I built a coffin from scrap lumber in the basement and dug, with Janice, his grave in the side yard. Soda weighed 160 pounds in his prime, large even for a sheepdog, and it took over seven hours to dig the hole in the rocky Connecticut soil. We placed his cold, stiff body in the ground, wrapped in his blanket and with articles of clothing that held each of our scents. Tears streaked the dirt on our faces as we ritualized our loss of Soda Pop with the Chippewa tradition of facing the four directions of the seasons and sprinkling tobacco over him, before filling the grave with the coldness of earth. Crocus and snowdrops adorn his grave each spring.

During the Vietnam years, the soldiers I counseled were fond of saying, "Keep the light," which meant, in its most literal sense, stay alive. It took me a while to realize they were telling me and each other to stay alive emotionally as well as physically.

I see myself as a keeper of the light, breathing life into smoldering ashes gasping to become vibrant flames. I use the passion-filled lantern of my own circular life and journey to guide my clients in finding the posts or stones that mark the boundaries and ends of their travel—teaching them, through my storytelling, to acknowledge each person, place, and event in the circles of their lives, to say goodbye as they pass by, and perhaps to linger for a while with each one.

Storytelling is my way of overcoming my clients' reticence to disclose their lives' significant points of termination and change. Through the telling of my stories of goodbyes, and the keeping of their stories and goodbyes by me, endings become beginnings and the circle remains alive. I am a keeper of the light.

Keep the light!

Chapter 4

Groups and the Velveteen Rabbit

Although I have been facilitating groups and teaching group courses since 1970, I still have difficulty explaining their effects on group members. Facilitated on the basis of established psychological theory and the leader's expertise and skill, process groups may be used in a proactive and preventive way to enhance and increase individuals' positive interactions and existing abilities, or in a remedial and educational manner to address the effects of negative life interactions and to teach members positive ways of interacting—providing them with faith in their ability to attain the more positive effects of human interactions.

Although process groups provide a more planned and systematic format than the process of living in which to focus on the effects of human interaction, groups are also unpredictable in terms of their effects. What may be a positive experience for one group member may be experienced as negative by another (both within and outside the group context). And, while one group member may be best facilitated by support, encouragement, and positive feedback, another may experience the greatest effects of the group by being pushed to confront uncomfortable and painful issues in his or her life and interactions. Experiencing pain may not always have a negative effect, just as receiving rewards may not always result in positive outcomes. As a group leader and educator, I most enjoy the fact that all groups and their members are somewhat different, even though members most often share commonalties in their individual development, and the group process progresses through similar stages of growth, to termination.

The unpredictability of groups, however, makes it difficult to define process group variables or to quantify and measure their outcomes. The process and interactions of different groups vary, and the outcomes and effects on group members also differ—positive for some and negative for others. Rarely, however, are the effects or outcomes of process groups neutral. People are affected by human interactions in groups, even though we cannot always predict how.

To make this point, I often use the example that most people do not have the opportunity to choose their family. No one asks us who we would like to choose as our parents or siblings. For some, the family group is positive and healthy. For others, families are dysfunctional, hurtful, negative, and traumatic group experiences. Families' effects are often random as well. Individuals who grow up in normal, healthy families may have significant problems, while others who are raised in dysfunctional families may develop into independent, competent, caring, strong, contributing members of society with few life issues, despite their family history. Some might even argue that it is the painful, uncomfortable, and difficult-to-overcome obstacles and experiences in life from which we learn and gain the most.

The role of process groups, however, is not as difficult. Groups play a significant role in our society and lives: families, work units, clubs, cliques and peer groups, gangs, education and classrooms, businesses and organizations, communities, group therapy, and so on. All of these groups include a process to some degree, regardless of their structure.

So, given the inevitable role that groups play in our lives and society, and given the outcome studies in support of the efficiency and effectiveness of therapy groups, what is the process of groups? We process our therapy sessions; we talk about the process of learning, development, change, and therapy, as if we know the meaning of process. But it is in groups, I believe, that we come closest to knowing the meaning of process (Freud 1929).

As a young counselor and therapist, I thought I had found a significant clue: nonverbal behavior. After all, Freud said, "Nonverbal behavior is leakage from the unconscious" (Freud 1929), although he also said, "Sometimes a cigar is just a cigar" (Freud 1929). In any event, I became a habitual observer in groups and elsewhere of nonverbal behaviors as the source of process and its meaning. The content of group members' spoken words increasingly became "white noise," as I scanned the group members for a glancing gaze, the movement of a foot or hand, the twisting of a wedding band, a heavy sigh, a shift in a seat, the twitch of a lip, a filled pause or hesitancy in a shaky voice. Indeed, this must be the process of groups.

I still believe nonverbal behavior to be part of the matrix. Through it all, however, it has come down to, quite simply, realizing that the process of groups is interaction (verbal and nonverbal): interaction between and among group members as well as with the group leader. The role of human interactions may be one of the most positive or traumatic aspects of our lives. Either way, human interactions may have the most significant and meaningful effects on personal development, self-concept and esteem, worldviews, and our ability to form significant personal and professional relationships. Many if not most of these interactions occur in a group context.

In short, process groups provide the forum and format for individuals to experience themselves; to address and explore the effects of life's negative interactions; to understand how others affect them and they affect others; and to learn new, healthier, and more positive ways of interacting and living. The importance of process groups lies in the fact that such group goals and planned effects are not always found or experienced in the natural, and often random, groups in which people find themselves.

At one point, I gave up on attempting to describe and explain process as it applies to the role and effect of groups, and therapy in general. Instead, I focused my attention on the structure of groups. In the structured components of groups I found variables that were potentially quantifiable. I even theorized distinct group modalities (task-process, socioprocess, and psychoprocess) with measurable variables as elements of their structure: group objective, focus, leader behavior, and member behavior and expectations. Likewise, other researchers and group experts have touted the positive effects and outcomes of structured process groups.

Alas, the process of groups remains elusive and nebulous. No matter what their structure, number and member composition, consistency of leader behavior and group procedures, or predictable group stages that unfold—each group is different. Although this aspect provides for ambiguity and frustration at times, it also makes each group different and exciting.

As an inevitable part of living, there will most likely never be the choice of not being involved in a group form of one type or another. Similarly, and more than likely, the scientific tools to objectively and quantifiably measure the salient and subjective aspects of process groups and outcome variables may not be developed and applied during my professional or, perhaps, personal lifetime.

This, in many ways, is the beauty of groups. Despite our attempts to define psychology as a science through application of the scientific method, objectivity, and quantification of human behavior, process groups remain unpredictable, subjective, qualitative, and a sort of art form. Just as not everyone has the ability and skill to be a scientist, not everyone possesses the artistic talents to be a group leader.

I still recall my first graduate course in group process. I was eager to learn how to be an effective, productive group member and, someday, to become an effective group leader. The very first thing the professor, who later became my group mentor, said to the class was, "The single most important factors in facilitating an effective group are the leader's authenticity and genuineness and the leader's belief in groups. As a leader, if you are not who you are and if you do not believe that groups affect people and their lives, then the groups you facilitate will be ineffective." I knew this was not going to be an easy course. As an early student of groups, I also did not want to hear a description of how to facilitate effective groups. I wanted it to be easy, systematic, orderly, and concrete. Besides, what if I lacked belief or group members did not like my authentic self?

After thirty years of facilitating, teaching, and studying such groups, I now better understand my mentor's statement.

Believing and having faith in the effects of group process is also consistent with perceiving process groups as an art form in which the leader and members may create and innovate as they go, demonstrating their faith in people and the process, as well as the leader's ability to construct and orchestrate growth-producing experiences and human interactions among group members.

Developing this faith and belief in groups and artistic ability as a group leader doesn't occur all at once. This too is a process. One of my own most significant experiences in this process of developing my belief and realness in groups occurred in 1978, three years after I completed my doctorate.

I was teaching an undergraduate psychology course in adolescent development at the University of Minnesota-Duluth. As was my custom, I used in-class discussion groups to illustrate the concepts and material the students were studying. During one of these in-class groups, a usually active student, Nan, looked distressed. She was a tall, lanky young woman, about twenty-two years old, with short brown hair, a pretty face, and an especially noticeable sparkle in her eyes.

This day her eyes didn't sparkle; they were distant and misty. I noticed that she looked faraway and pensive, and asked if the group could be of any help. She said the material we were studying—childhood and adolescent illnesses—was disturbing to her. With little probing, Nan disclosed to the group that she had had childhood leukemia, had gone through treatment, and had lost her hair during chemotherapy, but was now in remission.

Nan cried for a while after her disclosure to the group, and she and I talked in the hallway following the end of the class period. The next class meeting the sparkle had returned to her eyes and she thanked the group and me for listening to her and being supportive. The content of the class changed with the next reading assignments, and no one brought up the topic of Nan's leukemia in the group again, including me.

The long winter semester in Duluth dragged on and on. Nan stopped by my office occasionally during the semester, "just to talk for a while." Although I wanted to ask her how she was doing with the leukemia, during the group and in my office, I never did. I was not real with Nan, in the group or outside. I wasn't a very good "keeper of the light" at that point in my life. I did not tell her that issues of death were still very real for me; Vietnam seemed like only yesterday. I did not tell Nan that I was pushing her away to avoid my own pain surrounding death and loss. I did not tell her that I felt like crying during her group disclosure and when she stopped by my office, "just to talk for a while."

The dragging semester and adolescent development class ended, and I did not see Nan until early May, when she again showed up at my office door. She was in tears; her leukemia was no longer in remission.

Following her appearance at my door, Nan and I spent many afternoons sitting near the campus pond. Mostly I listened as she marveled at the wildflowers and butterflies, but I still was not real with her. I was listening when she told me, sitting next to the pond in early summer, that she was being admitted to University Hospital in Minneapolis the next week for a bone marrow transplant. She cried some more. I just listened and still was not real.

We hugged at parting and I told her I would visit her in the hospital. I didn't. Nan died later that summer; she never went home from the hospital after her transplant. Her sister brought to my office a ceramic candleholder that Nan had made for me before she died, and a note that said, "I miss sitting with you next to the pond." Tears began to well in my eyes, but Nan never saw them. I never told Nan goodbye, and I never told her the reason I did not visit her was because of my own pain and loss.

Nan taught me how to better "keep the light," and the importance of being real. Over the years, I have lost the note but not her words, and the candleholder she made for me sits unobtrusively on a small table. It's a reminder that showing others our real self and telling them how we feel about them, even when it is pain and hurt, may be the only way to be effective in our lives and in our relationships with others, in a group context or one-to-one.

I now trust that the group process will be an expression of our realness in interacting with others and that the effect will be meaningful for all of us. I do not know of anyone who has ever demonstrated conclusively the effectiveness of group therapy, or individual therapy for that matter. One develops a belief in group process and its effects by experiencing them as a group member or leader, not by studying, quantifying, and measuring discrete group variables. One creates an effective group by expressing one's realness and beliefs in interaction with others.

How does one evaluate and measure such expressions? Anyone who believes in process groups and their effectiveness realizes the answer to such a question can be found only by experiencing a group in which the leader and members are honest with themselves, real in their interactions with others, and believe that such experiences are effective in changing peoples' lives.

Although I have never disclosed it in a published forum, I now begin each new group I facilitate, and each new graduate class I teach, with the following passage from *The Velveteen Rabbit*:

> "What is REAL?" asked the Rabbit one day, when they were lying side by side near the nursery fender, before Nana come to tidy the room. "Does it mean having things that buzz inside you and a stick-out handle?"
>
> "Real isn't how you are made," said the Skin Horse. "It's a thing that happens to you. When a child loves you for a long time, not just to play with, but REALLY loves you, then you become Real."
>
> "Does it hurt?" asked the Rabbit.
>
> "Sometimes," said the Skin Horse, for he was always truthful. "When you are Real you don't mind being hurt."
>
> "Does it happen all at once, like being wound up," he asked, "or bit by bit?"
>
> "It doesn't happen all at once," said the Skin Horse. "You become. It takes a long time. That's why it doesn't often happen to people who break easily, or have sharp edges, or who have to be carefully kept. Generally, by the time you are Real, most of your hair has been loved off, and your eyes drop out and you get loose in the joints and very shabby. But these things don't matter at all, because once you are Real you can't be ugly, except to people who don't understand."
>
> "I suppose you are Real?" said the Rabbit. And then he wished he had not said it, for he thought the Skin

> Horse might be sensitive. But the Skin Horse only smiled." (Williams 1989, 18–23)

What is the role and effect of process groups? For her graduation, a student who had been a member of my graduate-level group courses gave me a copy of *The Polar Express* (Van Allsburg 1985) and a silver bell from Santa's sleigh. The last page of *The Polar Express* reads: "At one time most of my friends could hear the bell, but as the years passed, it fell silent for all of them. . . . Though I've grown old[er], the bell still rings for me as it does for all who truly believe."

Chapter 5

Day Storms and Night Dreams

When I was growing up in the Midwest, summer days were often a time of intense thunderstorms and, sometimes, unexpected and devastating tornadoes. Tornadoes rarely occur at night—I guess it has something to do with aspects of meteorology and weather forecasting about which I know little. I know that storms, day or night, are often unpredictable. When I was a young boy, spending hours playing sandlot baseball in a vacant field near my home, the hot, muggy summer days often spawned dark, ominous thunderclouds in the early afternoon. Those of us who played in the sandlot grew accustomed to the afternoon storms and were more concerned with the postponement or, worse yet, cancellation of our games than the intensity of pending turbulence.

That was before the afternoon the tornado appeared above the oak and maple trees of the nearby woods, and began its decent and sweep across the corn-planted muck fields, toward the man-made creek-culvert that separated the black-earth cornfields from our playing field. The thunderheads had rolled in as usual, and my fellow players and I were committed to finishing the last few innings of our daily game. But the sky was different and we were intent on ignoring it. It had turned a funny purplish-yellow; the clouds seemed darker, thicker, lower to the ground; and the temperature had changed, quickly, from its typical shirt-sticking mugginess to a chilling dankness that we felt beneath our already damp clothing.

It was almost upon us before we could assimilate the now-obvious clues to what was impending: the tornado funnel appeared over the trees, as if it had been hiding secretly among the giant trunks of the nearby oaks and maples. The sweeping motion of the funnel's tail was almost hypnotizing—like the back-and-forth movement of a pendulum—and we all stared at the turbulent swirlingness as if it were a mass of cotton candy on a paper stick. Finally someone, it may have been me, screamed, "Run for the house . . . the cellar!" Mine was the nearest house to the playing field, and there was an outside bulkhead that led to its dirt-floor cellar. The heavy, water-soaked, rotting doors of the bulkhead were thrown open as the less-than-nine-to-a-team sandlot players crowded down the four rickety steps and through the narrow doorway passage, and crouched and huddled in the cobweb-infested cellar that was barely more than a crawl space to a full-grown adult.

The sound of a tornado is similar to that of an approaching train, just as the old-timers had described it when they talked about the various storms they had lived through and cleaned up after. Arms and legs entwined, we waited as the sound of the locomotive tornado grew louder and nearer—until the breaking glass and thuds on the floor above our heads sounded as if we were sitting beneath a railroad trestle as the local Jackson-to-Lansing freight train passed overhead. It lasted only seconds, it seemed, from the roaring noise of a fast, oncoming locomotive to stone silence—an eerie shift in sensation and perception. No one moved. Maybe we thought the tornado was hiding again, like it had been hiding in the woods, and it would return as soon as we dared show ourselves at the bulkhead entrance to the cellar. Finally someone said, "I think it's gone," and one by one we ascended from the crawl space beneath the house. Amazingly, the sun was shining, as if nothing had happened, just another late summer day in the Midwest, although not as humid as usual. Also amazingly, the house was still standing, as were the huge box-elder trees that surrounded it. Most of the windows had been blown out; the screened back door was hanging by its spring, like a stretched tendon; and the chimney was gone from the roofline up, with its bricks neatly gathered in a pile close to the cellar bulkhead. Otherwise, just another less humid than usual, late summer day in the Midwest.

I don't remember how long I dreamed about this particular day storm. At night, the sound of a passing car in need of a new exhaust became the roar of the approaching funnel; and because the freight line tracks of the Jackson-to-Lansing train were less than fifty yards from my house, you can imagine what havoc could be created in my night dreams by an atypical nighttime freight run. Gradually, the intensity of that day storm faded and, along with it, the intensity of my night dreams associated with it.

Although the experience of that late summer tornado was one of the most *personally engaging* and *intense* of my tender years, as I grew older and experienced more intense weather, I became less fearful of day storms. However, day storms of another type, emotional ones, seemed to be increasing in intensity and frequency, as were their accompanying night dreams. But more of that later.

I have been fascinated with dreams and their meaning since my undergraduate years as a psychology major; my guess is that most therapists (aspiring or otherwise) share a similar fascination with the world of dreams. Over my past thirty years as a practicing therapist and educator of therapists, I have continued to form ideas about dreams and their meaning and place in our everyday lives. My thinking about dreams is the product of working with clients, teaching, and studying related research and scholarship that has focused on the unconscious, emotions and their intensity, and metaphoric versus literal thinking and communication.

There have always been two views of the unconscious: as a repository of negative ideas and as a positive force that guides people toward what is best for them. I have come to the belief that the unconscious, particularly as expressed in dreams, is a positive force that guides us toward what is best for us.

I have also concluded that the basic approach to almost all schools of psychotherapy is educational. What a therapist teaches may vary, but the fact that clients need to be educated appears to be a given. As such, therapists need to be personally involved and engaged with their clients, not neutral, and the main therapeutic task is that of educating—influencing and changing—our clients to enlarge their innovative solutions to life-problems. Such personal involvement with clients is often an intense educational and therapeutic experience that works at a relationship level, not at an awareness (conscious) level. That is, what happens in *personally involved* and *emotionally intense* therapeutic relationships can be so complex that conscious conceptualization as one works is unlikely.

I have also come to believe that dreams are part of an iterative series of unconscious emotions that the therapist must attempt to change by educating the client to be more imaginative and metaphoric. Therapy changes the emotional sequences themselves, or the client's interpretation of the emotional sequences, via the imagination, stories, fantasies, and metaphors of dreams.

In my teaching of therapists, I use metaphors, such as case examples and stories, to describe concepts, constructs, and client situations that are too complex for literal explanation. I believe that metaphor is the basis of all art, religion, myth, and dreams, and that it is the most emotionally laden form of communication and expression. Thus, a therapist who takes everything literally is limited and will miss most of the meaning of any communication in life, dreams or otherwise. Related to the notions of literal versus metaphoric thinking and communication is recent research in the workings of the brain and emotions—summarized briefly here.

A primer of the relevant research in this area (Goleman 1995) concerns two key parts of the primitive brain that gave rise to the cortex and neocortex (the thinking brain): the hippocampus and amygdala. In effect, according to Goleman (1995), these two parts of the brain have two memory systems, one for context (the hippocampus) and one for emotionally intense experiences (the amygdala). Emotional memories, stored in the hippocampus and amygdala, can have a mind of their own, independent of the rational, thinking brain. The amygdala, for example, does perceive and does remember. It is the repository of emotional impressions, memories, and responses—a "cognitive unconscious," if you will—outside the consciousness of our thinking brain. While our thinking brains and senses "stand down" during sleep, our emotional memories and reactions are left unconstrained. Similarly, the emotions and contexts stored in the cognitive unconscious, and not monitored by the literal and rational functions of the cortex and neocortex (the thinking brain), are free to arrange and express emotional impressions and reactions in metaphoric ways. That is, during our night dreams, and without the rational reasoning of the thinking brain, various emotional memories, responses, and contexts may become mixed and matched, intertwined, or blended in ways that create new stories and fantasies that are very different from our literal experience and interpretation of them while we are awake.

Given my continued work with dreams and recent research related to the brain and emotions, I now believe that many, if not all, of our emotional memories and reactions (psychological processes) are most likely imprinted, physical energy stored in the "cognitive unconscious" of the amygdala—expressed in dreams and flashbacks and immune to conscious control or elimination. Dreams are an unconscious positive force in our lives—not necessarily an indicator of disorder, neurosis, or psychosis—that guides us toward what is best for us. Night dreams are as real as our cognitive, daytime awareness, and therapists must learn what these fantasies and metaphoric, moralistic dream stories communicate about their clients—and about themselves.

Two clinical examples may serve to illustrate the metaphoric, cognitively unconscious, and positive force of night dreams in the resolution of emotionally laden and intense day storms; both of them involve Vietnam and combat veterans. The first involves an experience while I was teaching a group class in Iowa during the late 1970s. I was demonstrating the use of "guided fantasies" as a group work technique. To demonstrate the technique, I had the class members lie on the floor in the group room, with their eyes closed, while I began with a relaxation exercise before taking them on the guided fantasy. Members were very relaxed and sleepy in the darkened room. I then provided the guided fantasy about a wizard, sitting on top of a mountain, who had the answers to our most pressing life-questions. The fantasy also involved a leisurely walk through a beautiful wood on the way to the top of the mountain and the wise wizard. Unbeknownst to me, one of the class members was a Vietnam combat veteran. When the fantasy was completed and members were guided back from the fantasy to the context of the group room, he continued to lie on the floor with his eyes closed. He did not respond to auditory or tactile stimulation for a few more moments—he was in a catatonic-like state. Gradually—it seemed like forever—he opened his eyes and he was visibly shaking. He said, "I went back to Vietnam." The class took a break so he and I could talk. We decided it would be best if he went home rather than return to class. A few days later, he dropped by my office and told me of how he had somehow, during a dream, integrated the positive aspects of the guided fantasy with some of the traumatic events he had experienced in Vietnam. In his dream, he had metaphorically created a new story for his intense emotional memories of Vietnam, and stopped having daytime flashbacks.

Some two or three years later, I was teaching a course in a paraprofessional training program for Native Americans in Minnesota. One young man taking the course wore a neck pendant depicting the black outline of a tiger's head etched into cream-colored ivory. When I casually asked him about the significance of the pendant, he told me of an experience he had had as a combat veteran in the jungles of Vietnam. He had become separated from his unit during a firefight and was left alone in the jungle as night approached. He hid in the underbrush all night, as enemy soldiers walked near where he lay beneath the cover of the jungle and darkness. Exhausted, he had fallen asleep. He dreamed that a tiger had come from deep within the jungle and lain down beside him while he slept. In his dream, he awakened to find the tiger beside him, like a sentinel guarding over him. The tiger told him, not in words but in some other way, that he was safe and would be found soon by his unit. Early the next morning his unit found and returned him, unharmed, to the base camp. While telling this story, the young man implied that he was no longer certain if the tiger had been real or a dream, but it didn't matter. Although he was afraid in the hostile jungles of Vietnam, he had listened to the protecting "dream-tiger" and remained calm until his unit found him. He now wore the tiger pendant—a metaphor for the experience and the need for calm in his life. At times of stress and pending panic, the metaphoric night dream of the jungle and tiger would return to calm and guide him through the experience of emotionally intense day storms.

I would like to return to my own emotionally laden day storms and the ideas of *personal involvement, emotional intensity*, and *education* (therapy) as they relate to my conceptualization of the world of dreams.

In my more philosophical moments, I believe we have certain lessons to learn, and that these lessons keep presenting themselves to us (like our emotions) until we have learned them adequately. And, very often, these lessons are taught in our night dreams, as well as during our waking hours. In my own life, as I have reflected on this abstraction over the years, some thematic and recurring situations have created emotional day storms and helped me to learn. These iterative themes may be nothing more than coincidence or the random occurrence of life-events. Regardless, and as reflected in the clinical examples, one of the recurring patterns in my own life has been that of war and its aftermath in the lives of those with whom I grew up, loved, and have worked as a therapist and educator.

My father entered World War II in 1942; returning from the 101st Airborne Division, D-Day, Normandy, Bastogne, Paris, and Berlin, more than three years later. I was a post-World War II baby, and the people in my small Midwestern town called my dad a drunk. All I knew and believed, until I entered adolescence, was that my father was a war hero and the recipient of two silver stars and had been the subject of an article about his bravery in the January 1945 issue of *Life* magazine. There was emotional turbulence in my family before I entered adolescence, however, memories of which are still imprinted in my cognitive unconscious and about which I still occasionally have night dreams. One in particular occurred when I was about seven years old.

It was a snowy winter evening, with my family sitting at the kitchen table, when my sister and her husband-to-be announced to my father that she was pregnant. He had been drinking heavily and became enraged at the news. He followed my sister and her young man to the driveway as they were leaving in the midst of the emotional storm. Although the driver's side window of the 1951 Ford was raised, my father tried to strike the young man with his fist, putting his hand through the window instead. The young man sped down the driveway, dragging my father alongside the car with his hand caught in the broken class of the window. Some twenty-five yards later the car stopped under the streetlight, tumbling my father to the ground, and then raced out of sight. My brother, who was fourteen, grabbed a towel from the bathroom, ran to where my father lay, tourniqueted his arm, and carried him the twenty-five yards back to the family car. The police stopped us just outside the hospital entrance because we had bolted through every stoplight on Main Street, regardless of its color. No tickets were issued for the stoplight violations or my brother's under-age driving.

What I remember most, though, is the scene at the hospital and the following ambulance ride to the Ann Arbor Veterans Hospital. Our local hospital was an old, four-story brick structure, the kind with high ceilings and globe lights attached to slow-turning ceiling fans suspended twelve feet above the two-foot-square black-and-white floor tiles. I could see into the emergency room, whose door had been left open during the frantic activity of attending to my father, to just past where the nurse sat at the huge wooden desk, in her white-starched uniform and pointed hat, guarding the entrance to the bowels of the hospital. I saw the blood squirt from my father's hand onto the high ceiling, and I closed my eyes as the doctors "tied off" the bleeding artery in his wrist. My fear turned to excitement as the ambulance left the hospital for Ann Arbor, with my mother and me sitting in the back with my father. I fell asleep watching the reflection of the ambulance's flashing red light echo off the roadway and highway signs, dreaming of fire trucks, police cars, and ambulances. My father lost eighty percent use of his right hand, and my mother and I made weekly trips to Ann Arbor for several months to come.

But the most significant events of emotional intensity occurred between my father and me during my adolescence. Until then, I avoided most of the emotional day storms of my father and family by playing baseball in the sandlot near my home and fantasizing and dreaming about playing third base for the Detroit Tigers, with Al Kaline, Harvey Kuenn, Rocky Colavito, Denny McLain, Mickey Lolich, John Hiller, Stormin' Norman Cash, Mickey Stanley, Willie Horton, and Bill Freehan. As I grew older, my father's "war stories"—usually told in a drunken stupor—became tiresome to me, and I began telling him so. The emotional intensity and conflict between us escalated, sometimes resulting in physical as well as emotional expression. So, once again, I avoided my father and my home situation by immersing myself in high school athletics and academics rather than in fantasies and dreams. I structured my academic and athletic activities in such a manner that I rarely saw my father; he did not object.

There was another day storm of the weather kind during my time in the military, this one a hurricane. Hurricane Camille struck the Gulf Coast of the United States in the fall of 1969, while I was stationed in Biloxi, Mississippi. Most of us assigned there spent the next six months cleaning up after the devastation of the storm. This was also my first direct experience with death—other than Gramma Pearl—searching for missing persons and finding them dead in the back bay waters of the Gulf.

After I was discharged from the military and completed my doctoral studies, the night dreams began. All the memories imprinted during the emotionally intense day storms of the first thirty years of my life seemed to seek expression simultaneously. At the time, I did not see the night dreams as a positive force guiding me toward what was best for me.

Instead, I dreaded the approach of night, sleep, and dreams. I would often postpone sleep to the point of exhaustion and actively tried to forget any night dreams or parts of them. But, I was aware, at some level, that my night dreams were mostly about my father, the soldiers of Vietnam whom I had counseled, and weather-type storms.

After a summer visit from my father in northern Minnesota, I stopped trying to avoid sleep and the night dreams. At first, my night dreams were horrifying, frightful, dreadful experiences. When I woke up, I would be left with only the intense emotional traces of the dreams and no conscious memory of their content or context. Gradually, a metaphor emerged: my father and me sitting on a bench at the Duluth, Minnesota, Harbor on Lake Superior, near the Aerial Bridge that connects the city to Lake Island. This was an actual event; what follows is the metaphoric story.

As we sat on a bench on the harbor, each drinking Canadian beer and eating Wisconsin cheese, staring into the waters of Lake Superior, and talking softly, we occasionally turned our heads to face each other and smile. The metaphor gradually expanded to include me sitting on the same bench in the same place with one of the many combat soldiers whom I had counseled during Vietnam. Sometimes the metaphor changed somewhat, and my father would be sitting on the bench with one of the Vietnam veterans. In all of the metaphors, however, the people were talking softly and smiling as they stared into the expanse of Lake Superior, occasionally turning to look at each other. The last element to be added to the metaphoric night dream was a severe storm that gathered over the lake (a "nor'easter"), gaining in intensity and force as it approached and overcame the harbor and the two people sitting on the bench. Intense waves

Chapter 6

Oz Never Gave to the Tin Man

When you are in the middle of a story it isn't a story at all, but only a confusion; a dark roaring, a blindness, a wreckage of shattered glass and splintered wood; like a house in a whirlwind, or else a boat crushed by the icebergs or swept over the rapids, and all aboard powerless to stop it. It's only afterwards that it becomes anything like a story at all. When you are telling it, to yourself or to someone else.

— Margaret Atwood, *Alias Grace*

It was past midnight in October 1971; I sat in the intensive care unit of Fitzsimmons Army Hospital; my six-week-old son, Ross, was lying in an incubator a foot from my chair, clear plastic tubes protruding from his small nose and two "cutdowns" on his tiny head and ankle. I cradled my forehead in the palms of both my hands, my face downward toward the floor. I watched as the tears dropping from my eyes splashed in gathering puddles on the checkered-tile floor. A hand touched my slumped shoulder and a soft voice said, "Courage, courage, my son."

I mumbled to the floor, "Courage, courage. What the fuck does courage have to do with this?" I slowly lifted my head, turning it sideways and backward to see the cross-insignia and the silver oak leaf on the chaplain's dress blues. The three chevrons on the sleeves of my own khaki uniform were hidden beneath the cover of my green hospital gown. I asked him, again, "What the fuck does courage have to do with this?"

He didn't answer. Instead, he asked me if my son had been baptized and if I wanted to pray. "Will courage keep my son alive? Will praying keep my son alive? Yes, my son has been baptized; will that keep him alive? I apologize for saying fuck, Colonel. Now, sir, would you please leave us alone?"

I don't think that courage when we have no choice is the same as courage when we can choose to be courageous or not. I had no choice during my son's illness, but courage did have something to do with it.

Following the chaplain's hasty departure, I stood and reached my arm and surgical-gloved hand through the circular membrane on the side of my son's incubator. I gently touched the sole of his foot, the one with the cutdown and plastic tubing feeding fluid into his body. I caressed the hollow of his back and felt his shallow, weak breaths. I wanted to feel him, skin to skin. But without the surgical glove I would risk infecting him, so I followed the rules. With the courage that connected the pulse of Ross's diminutive heart to mine, I whispered to him—and to myself, "I love you, Rossi. I love you so much. Stay alive if you can, Rossi; stay alive if you can. I'm sorry I didn't take care of you. I'm sorry I won't be able to be your father. I'm sorry you won't be able to be my son. I'm sorry, Rossi; I love you." The doctors believed it would be a miracle if he lived through the night; his prognosis for survival was less than twenty percent, and even if he did live, there was a higher than fifty percent chance he would be mentally retarded.

I left the hospital shortly after saying goodbye to my son, and drove my '66 Mustang around the city of Denver until sunrise; I wasn't ready for the hospital's phone call about my son's fate. One of the places I drove was to the University of Denver, where I was studying part-time for my Ph.D. in the evenings, during my off-duty hours from the military. I parked the car in a dark, secluded area of a vacant lot. In the past, universities were always places of safety and security for me, places of comfort and peacefulness. As I sat looking into the darkness, I kept thinking to myself, "Why didn't you take off that fucking glove and touch him the way you wanted? Why didn't you just touch him the way you wanted?" I didn't have the courage to break the rules, even though I knew in my heart what I wanted to do.

When I returned home at dawn, my wife said there was still no news from the hospital. I called my parents back in Michigan to tell them what was happening. Although I have long since excused my father for the comment, his response was, "Well, you'll just have to make a new one." In fact, in the intervening years, I have come to value and honor my father's directness, his no-bullshit honesty—a result of all the adversity in his own life, and his courage, I think.

After I hung up the phone with my parents, I went to my son's room, closed the door, knelt at the side of his empty crib, and prayed. I bargained with "God." I would give my life to "Him" if "He" would only spare my son. As an aside, I saw a movie recently in which one of the main—and mentally challenged—characters, following the death of his beloved dog, went to his church to pray for his dog's soul. Looking at the crucifix hanging at the front of the sanctuary, the distraught, mentally challenged man looked at the priest standing nearby and said, "If I were God, I wouldn't have let them do that to my son." Although I laughed at this line from the movie, I think—at the time—it would have reflected my true and honest feelings toward "God." But I was desperate, alone in my pain and grief, helpless, and I believed I was without courage—so I bargained.

After showering and shaving, I returned to the intensive care unit of the Army hospital and the smiles of the attending nurses. My son was better, still not out of danger, but much better. Ross remained in the ICU for another three weeks and was finally released to the home care of his mother and me. I went back to my duty assignment—which, ironically, was located in the same hospital—an unwilling airman and counselor for returning Vietnam combat veterans. No one in my unit was much interested in hearing of my son's plight and recovery—rightly so, perhaps, given the tragedies we encountered with our soldier-clients and the young men dying in the jungles of Vietnam each day. So I stopped talking about my son with them, and everyone else, and retreated into silence.

My marriage was fragile and strained, and, rightly or wrongly, I blamed my wife for my son's illness. Since his birth and before his admission to ICU, she had been breast-feeding him. He had not been gaining weight as I thought he should, although the doctors saw no reason for concern or alarm during his periodic checkups. I pleaded with her and the doctors to supplement his feeding with baby formula, to no avail. I always checked him one last time before going to bed myself each night. The night of our emergency rush to the hospital, I found him in his crib, an ashen bluish-gray color, barely breathing, looking into my eyes with a vacant, distant stare. In the hospital emergency room, the attending physician said he was dehydrated and malnourished, with an almost nonexistent blood-sugar count. His haunting "cat's cry," as labeled by the doctor, indicated that his tiny brain was starving for nutrition; the damage had probably already been done. In an attempt to reassure us, the physician said, "These things happen with young babies really quickly, in a matter of hours sometimes. It's good you found him when you did. We'll do everything we possibly can."

It doesn't take courage to blame someone else; courage comes with owning, accepting, and acknowledging one's own responsibility and accountability. Without courage, I blamed my wife, although I think the damage to the marriage had been done years before. Although married for three years before my son's birth, my wife and I had been high school sweethearts and in an exclusive yet tumultuous relationship since the age of thirteen—exclusive on my part anyway; her one premarital infidelity was a source of my own insecurity and mistrust in the marriage.

After my son's return home, my wife and I began marital counseling with our minister; he was holding me to my bargain with "God," which I had told him of in a one-to-one session soon after my son's release from the hospital. Through counseling, I took my fifty percent—no more and no less—of the blame, accountability, and responsibility for what had happened to my son, and for my role in the marriage. My affection and love, however, were another matter. I had not bargained with that, and all of it was devoted to my son, and only my son. I entered what I now call my "Jesus period," handing out tracts on the streets of Denver, "praising the Lord," proselytizing, and seeking to save the nonbelievers. Upholding my end of my deal with "God."

At night, lying on my back in bed and looking at the small, perforated holes in the acoustic ceiling tiles, I dreaded my life and the life I was to lead, the existential angst that was at times overwhelming. This too was something I kept to myself, without the courage to share it with my wife or in our counseling sessions with the minister. But, in my defense, neither of them wanted to hear such things. They didn't want to hear about my fear, my dread, my lingering pain, my unhappiness, and my anger—my anger. The goal of the minister's counseling was to keep us together and married, and the "problem" was mine: my blaming, my emotional distance, my disconnection from my wife. Each session focused on how I was doing with my problems. Had I overcome the blaming yet? Was there forgiveness in my heart? Did my wife notice any improvement in my expression of affection toward her? Were we doing family things together? Was my faith in "God" still strong? We ended each session in prayer, the minister asking "God" to heal Mike.

Perhaps I was therapy-wise, due to my own training and experience as a therapist, and resistive to the process and goals of the therapy being provided. Nevertheless, the experience was not a positive one for me, and I developed some very negative attitudes and feelings toward "pastoral" counseling. I also learned an important lesson about the harmful impact of the therapist's imposition of his or her own goals in therapy, and I swore to myself that this was a pitfall I would always try to avoid as a therapist.

"Courage, courage, my son." The lesson being taught in marital therapy, however, was that it took courage to be kind and forgiving, to endure and brave the adversities of my life.

So I went along to get along. For some, this may very well be a helpful notion of courage. For me, however, this form of courage ("Courage, courage, my son")—applied to my life adversities and feelings—was damning. I pretended; I pretended to be kind and forgiving; I pretended the wounds were healed and that I had not only endured but overcome my "problems."

I now know differently. If you think you can get through life without adversity, you're mistaken. The biggest lie I told was the lie I told to myself. It takes more courage to be honest and direct—with yourself and others—than to be kind. Insincere kindness can be the lie that steals your soul. I numbed myself emotionally and psychologically with everyone except Ross. In retrospect, the most dreadful aspect of my lie is that no one seemed to notice it was a lie—including me. I was either very good at deception and lying—a great pretender—or I was giving people (my wife, our minister-counselor, our families) what they wanted me to give: the courage to forgive, to endure, and to go along. It was more than I had to give; the courage, the kindness, and the forgiveness were false and insincere, a lie.

During the next two years, my son and I became inseparable. I bathed him, played with him, changed his diapers, taught him to pee (like daddy) in his training potty, rode my bicycle with him strapped securely in the carrier attached to my back, fed him, lay on the couch with him sleeping on my chest instead of putting him to bed. He straddled the old canister vacuum cleaner, like a cowboy riding a bronco, as I cleaned the house on Saturday mornings. Having a master's degree in counseling—and studying part-time in the evenings for my Ph.D. at the University of Denver—I had a working knowledge of child development and developmental tasks.

With discretion and unbeknownst to others, I would check Ross's gross- and fine-motor skills more than occasionally, asking him to pick up a button from the floor or the Cheerios accidentally spilled on the kitchen table, or asking him to retrieve my coins from the coffee table. I loved him, snuggled him, hugged him, kissed him—he became my life, the string that held fast to my heart and soul. He was the only part of my life that was not a lie.

I was discharged from the military in 1973 and we returned to Michigan, where I began teaching high school during the day and pursuing my doctorate in counseling in the evenings. Life seemed better. Denial and distortion are such wonderful defenses and require no courage. There was no overt conflict in the marriage, and I thought it to be as good as, maybe better than, many others I had observed or encountered. I resigned myself that to ask for or to want more from life was selfish and unwarranted. My son was beautiful, with no apparent harm done by his serious, near-fatal illness, confirmed by his pediatrician, who was aware of his medical history and who examined him for any problematic signs as a routine part of his regular appointments. Ross continued to be the center of my life and my universe.

Gradually, I stopped going to church and came out of my "Jesus period," becoming less and less willing to go along, to deny, and to distort, making more and more of my own choices, as I began to feel better about myself through the validation of the high school kids I was teaching and by my professors at the university, for "being myself." My existential angst returned, but this time I let it be instead of pushing it away with religion, lies to myself and others, and pretending. I was no longer willing to please others at my own expense; I began to question things: Was there a "God"? If there was no "God," was my bargain valid and my debt still due? If I could not live a genuine, authentic, and honest life myself, then how could I ask my clients to do so—without being a hypocrite? Although I still held parts of myself back and hidden from others, the courage to be myself was growing.

No longer religious or a churchgoer, I returned to the spirituality of a Native heritage: the harmony and balance among mind, body, and spirit (heart). I no longer proselytized Christianity or tried to save lost souls. Instead, I tried to live what was in my heart and to have the courage to express it honestly, and, in this way, hold true to my promise and bargain with a greater spirit.

In the spring before I completed my doctoral studies, my major professor asked me to be one of ten group facilitators for a large counselor training conference he conducted each year. I agreed and was pleased that he thought enough of me to ask. During the afternoon of each of the five days of the conference, attendees broke out into small process groups, for which I was one of the leaders. At the end of the conference, and following several pleasant and engaging interactions with one of the group members—both within and outside the context of the group process—she gave me the following poem:

Snow on Top of a Mountain

People to people
Person to person
Snow on top of a mountain
I wish it wasn't
so hard
You're made of many beautiful
unique parts
You're cold and yet so soft
and you can only melt

if you're around someone
warm
. . . And, so . . . far away
I'd like to climb up there
and make snowballs and
snowmen
But I can't . . . because,
you see . . . it's too far,
and I'm afraid of
high places
Besides, by the time I
climbed all that way
It would be summer
and you would be gone

Thanks Mike
You were helpful,
Love, Jan

In a matter of five short days, with the honesty of her heart and her poem, she had pierced my weakening façade, seeing the internal struggles and outward contradictions. We spent the remainder of that spring afternoon together. We walked together and talked about our goals and dreams in life, our families, our spouses, our children (she had three), our doubts and frustrations, her physically and emotionally abusive husband and unhappy marriage—our attraction to one another. But I denied my unhappiness in my marriage when she asked, and talked of Ross: my love for him and being his father. I know she saw through my denial of an unhappy marriage as well, but she didn't push the issue.

We ended the day by saying we should stay in touch professionally. By the time I completed my fifteen-minute drive home from the conference, I was no longer in denial. When I entered the house, I looked at my wife and said, "Let's go sit on the porch; I need to talk." I showed her the poem, cried, told her how unhappy I was in our relationship, and said that I had very strong feelings for Jan. Her response was, "Well, I owe you one; do what you have to do." I couldn't believe what I had heard. So much for honesty and directness, I thought. I said nothing more, except, "I think we should go back into counseling."

The next week we entered therapy again, this time with a female clinical social worker at the community mental health center. Once again, I was the one with the "problem": my unhappiness in the marriage, my feelings for Jan, my overattachment to Ross, my emotional detachment from my wife. Each week in therapy, I felt pummeled, grilled, coerced, accused, and criticized by the two of them, for whom I was and what I felt. Déja vu! The negative attitudes and feelings I experienced during pastoral counseling were now transferred to clinical social workers as well. Who the hell was training these people, anyway? Was this how most therapists did therapy? So much for listening, positive regard, caring, empathy, and authenticity for these folks.

Once again, I lost the courage to be honest and direct, in the therapy sessions and outside of them. I began to say what they wanted to hear, to please them. Each night, staying up late to prepare my lesson plans for teaching or to study, I read Jan's poem before going to bed. Jan called me at my university office one afternoon, as I was putting the finishing touches on my dissertation, and said she would like to see me—and I wanted to see her. We spent the next day together at the university, again talking for hours with one another.

I withdrew from therapy, although my wife continued. My willingness to sit in the client's chair was severely diminished as a result of these two experiences in therapy. To this day, my unwillingness to enter therapy remains—a powerful outcome and a lesson and awareness that are ever-present in my providing therapy to others.

I graduated in August, took my first postdoctoral position, and moved to Ohio with my wife and son. It took me another year to leave the marriage, although that was not the difficult choice. The courage of choice was to leave my son; it was the single most difficult choice I have ever made in my life, I think. I still have regrets and feel guilt sometimes, although he and I have reestablished a strong, loving, and close father-son relationship. I regret the brutal custody battle I initiated; I regret that I missed being there for him as he grew up; I regret that I was not the father for him that I wished to be and never had myself; I regret that he felt abandoned by me; I regret the periods of estrangement and conflict between us; I regret that I broke his heart; I regret that Janice (she has been "Janice" to me, instead of Jan, since our being together these past twenty-six years) lost custody of her own three children because she refused to please the court and presiding judge by saying that our relationship was "merely a one-night stand, a roll in the hay, a one-time affair."

I recall in particular one visitation with our children while Janice and I were teaching and living in Iowa. She and I were sitting by the swimming pool of our apartment complex as the children splashed about and played in the water. Ross, who was about six years old at the time, climbed from the edge of the pool, walked to where Janice and I sat, and said, "Dad, what about me, what the hell about me? Didn't you think about me when you divorced Mom?" With the same casualness with which he had approached us and asked his question, he turned, not waiting for a response, walked back to the edge of the pool, and dived into the water to play. My heart was in my stomach. His was a statement, not a question. I had it coming, and I valued his honesty and courage—as painful as it was to hear.

Despite the times of estrangement and conflict between us, during the years since I chose to leave, we have both mustered the courage over and over again to withstand the extremes of happiness at saying hello and the sadness and tears at saying goodbye to one another. He graduated from college cum laude and is now a high school teacher. In moments of shared morbid humor, we have said to one another that he probably would have been a genius if not for the brain damage as a baby, but he had to settle for being normal. We have also talked about what a wonderful young man he turned out to be, and credited his mom for her love and nurturing as a single parent.

At Christmas in 1998, he gave me the framed lyrics of a 1970 Neil Young song, "Old Man," that he had typed while listening to the music. Some of those lyrics include:

> Old Man, take a look at my life, I'm a lot like you were. . . .
> Live alone in a paradise that makes me think of two
> Love lost, such a cost, give me things that won't get lost
> Like a coin that won't get tossed, rollin' home to you
> Old Man, take a look at my life, I'm a lot like you were. . . .
> I've been first and last, look at how the time goes past
> But, I'm alone at last, rollin' home to you. . . .
> Old Man take a look at my life, I'm a lot like you were. . . .

During a visit with him in Michigan the following spring, I gave him an antique silver dollar, with the accompanying words:

> Son,
>
> Old Man, look at my life, I'm a lot like you were. . . .
>
> Old Man, look at my life, twenty-four and there's so much more
>
> Live alone in a paradise that makes me think of two
>
> Love lost, such a cost, give me things that don't get lost
>
> Like a coin that won't get tossed, rollin' home to you. . . .
>
> Old Man, look at my life, I'm a lot like you were. . . .
>
> I want you to have this 1886 Silver Dollar coin, Ross:
>
> No more love lost son;
>
> Like a coin that won't get tossed, rollin' home to you. . . .
>
> Pops (*Edutsi,* Cherokee for "Old Man")

Moments of courage, to me, come from the heart. Although I am not presumptuous enough to critique the wonderful messages of *The Wizard of Oz,* I nonetheless think it is the Tin Man, and the Tin Man's heart, rather than the bravery of the Cowardly Lion that best exemplifies courage. In the moments in which courage is required, be they times of adversity or choice, it is the matters of the heart that will determine our courage: our courage to face the adversities of life that inevitably will come; the courage to face ourselves—our frailties, errors, mistakes, weaknesses, and lies; the courage to be honest and true to ourselves and to our feelings and thoughts, though they may be painful and hurtful to others; the courage to express honestly what is in our heart.

I think most everyone has the capacity for courage. Unfortunately, in some instances, persons who have the courage to be honest and truthful are described instead as rude, unduly harsh or cruel, abusive, and even crazy or insane. The present expectations and norms for dishonesty, deceit, false politeness and kindness, and manipulation are so strong and prevalent.

Not long ago, after watching *Titanic* for the first time, I looked at Janice and said, "Ours is a love story, isn't it?" She smiled and replied, "Yes, yes, Michael, it is." I thought about what the chaplain had said to me so many years ago, sitting next to my son in the intensive care unit of the Army hospital in Denver: "Courage, courage, my son." And I thought of the lyrics sung by Dewey Bunnell in a 1975 *America* album: "Oz never did give nothing to the Tin Man, that he didn't, didn't already have. . . . Oh, Oz never did give nothing to the Tin Man . . . that he didn't, didn't already have": Courage, courage of the heart, the courage of truth and honesty in the love songs of an old man's heart.

Chapter 7

Cat's in the Cradle

I awoke early on a Saturday morning, unusual for me, a late sleeper. Drinking the first cup of coffee with Janice, we sat in the windowed, breakfast nook of our little, colonial house in Northern Minnesota watching the finches and mourning doves nibble their morning seed. She looked at me and said, "You need to go home, to see your father."

"Yeah, I know."

"No, Michael, now!"

"Now?"

Less than two hours later, the truck had been packed and gassed up, and we were headed toward the Upper Peninsula of Michigan and the five hundred miles of road leading to my father. Although Janice's premonitions are sometimes enigmatic to me (she is uncanny in her intuitive knowing and sensing), I did not question the need to see my father; he was dying, and she knew it. There was a sense of silent urgency as we traveled.

The truck's ashtray was full when we pulled into the driveway of my father's house in the late summer dusk. My mother greeted us at the porch door with tear-filled eyes. My older brother sat slouched and bleary-eyed in an overstuffed chair of the living room. My father was in his bedroom, sleeping restlessly. Cautiously, I opened the sliding accordion door to his room. The fixed stare of his eyes changed to a slight glimmer and a frail smile crossed his lips as he saw me standing in the narrow doorway.

"Hey Skeeter, come to see your old man?" I sat on the edge of his bed, as he reached for and grasped my hand. "Come to see me, come to see me one last time."

He wanted to get out of bed and go into the living room to be with everyone. Despite my protest that he remain in bed, I helped him up and we both managed somehow to squirm through the slim passageway of the bedroom, arm-in-arm, and arrive at the living room sofa. He grew more and more agitated with pain as the evening passed. My mother and brother, exhausted from alternating shifts of round-the-clock care and vigilance, accepted my offer to relieve them and went off to bed. Janice, also spent from the five-hundred-mile trip, departed to the truck's camper for some sleep as well.

My father and I spent the next eight hours saying goodbye: the good, the bad, and the ugly of it. We had made peace with each other some three years earlier, but there remained the need, one last time, to rehash and forgive the harm, conflict, and turbulence of the first thirty-two years of our father-son relationship. We talked, we listened, we cried; we laughed together, we held each other, and I rubbed his back as he lay on the floor, atop the sofa cushions.

"It's okay, it's okay, Dad. It's okay to sleep . . . it's okay to leave now . . . I love you." Those were my last words to him.

As dawn approached, and he drifted in and out of fitful sleep, I walked into the kitchen, joining the rest of the family at the table. From where I sat, I could see my father lying on the cushions in the living room. My brother and mother were discussing whether to readmit him to the hospital; he had become too much a burden for them to continue to care for at home. As I watched from my vantage at the kitchen table, my father slowly closed his eyes, sighed ever so slightly, and died. With tears in my eyes, I looked at them both and said, "There's no need for this discussion; Dad's gone."

Despite the family's earlier efforts to convince my sister to return from Texas, with numerous phone calls during the course of the evening and night, she insisted it was just another false alarm, and that she could not possibly get away on such short notice. Although my father loved Janice dearly in her own right, when she awoke on the morning of his death and entered the living room, he said, "Hey Sis. God, I'm glad you made it home in time." Unselfishly and without the blink of an eye, Janice immediately said, "Hey, Dad, of course I'm here," and played the role of my sister until my father died.

I gave the eulogy at my father's funeral. The centerpiece of that eulogy included lines from the lyrics of a song that brought tears to my eyes the first time I heard them, because they described much of our years and times together, what was and what could have been:

> And the cat's in the cradle and the silver spoon
> Little boy blue and the man in the moon
> "When you comin' home, Dad?"
> "I don't know when,

But we'll get together then, son, you know we'll have a good time then."
". . . I'm gonna be like you, dad, you know I'm gonna be like you."
And the cat's in the cradle and the silver spoon
Little boy blue and the man in the moon
"When you comin' home, son?"
"I don't know when,
But we'll get together then, Dad, you know we'll have a good time then."
. . . And the cat's in the cradle and the silver spoon
Little boy blue and the man in the moon
. . . Well he came from college just the other day
So much like a man I just had to say,
"Son, I'm proud of you
Can you sit for awhile?"
. . . He'd grown up just like me
My boy was just like me. . .
"When you comin' home, son?"
"I don't know when
But we'll get together then, Dad, you know we're gonna have a good time then . . ."

—Chapin, Kewley, and Chapin, *Cat's in the Cradle*

A 1945 article about my father had been published in *Life* magazine, which I showed to all of my boyhood friends. Part of it read:

> In addition to our regular weapons we all carried .45 pistols. Wilbur was the only one of us taking an M-1 rifle, the rest of us chose the Tommy gun for more firepower. We tried to talk him out of the M-1 but we knew it would be nice to have him along with it.

> Wilbur has the reputation of being pretty accurate with that gun and is famous for never shooting at a man unless he can aim dead center for the head. He doesn't miss. (Engel 1945, 75)

I didn't use this excerpt in his eulogy. It was no longer an apt description of him when he died in 1981.

Despite my preadolescent hero worship of my father, there was much emotional maelstrom in my family, memories of which still remain. Although I did not experience the trauma of combat myself, as a counselor of combat veterans during the Vietnam War, I felt traumatized vicariously by the atrocities, experiences, and emotions of war they conveyed to me. Sometimes I thought it was the second of my vicarious war traumatizations, the first being my father's experience in World War II.

There was an occasion on which our paths crossed in one of my most emotionally extreme and intense physical experiences. Somewhere between boyhood and adolescence, I had lost all respect for my father. I was embarrassed by him. At the beginning of my junior year of high school, returning home from school early one fall afternoon, I found my father slumped on the back porch, propped against the side of the house. The town sheriff had dumped him on the porch, rather than putting him in jail, following a mid-day bar fight in which he had taken the brunt of the abuse. Blood was trickling from above one eye, over the side of his nose and upper lip. Thinking he was unconscious, I quipped, barely audibly, "Mr. Boston got his ass kicked again." Unbeknownst to him, I often referred to my father as "Mr. Boston," in reference to the brand name of the cheap whiskey he drank. He heard my comment and uncoiled like a striking rattler. The fist of his crippled right hand struck me square in the mouth, fragments of my four front teeth splintering and falling to the porch's cement floor. Because he was off balance from his powerful swing, I was able to push him from the porch. He landed awkwardly on his right shoulder, breaking his collarbone. Incredibly, he scrambled to his feet, again charging me. I was able to step from the porch as his waist-high tackle pummeled me to the ground. With both his knees pinning my shoulders to the ground, despite the broken collarbone, he raised his fisted right hand once more for yet another blow to my already swollen face. His eyes were filled with rage as I stared into them with panic and fear. Then he pushed off my chest with his left hand and stood over me briefly, before turning and walking to the house. As I lay on my back on the ground I felt grateful for his act of mercy, knowing what he could have done to me if he had chosen to.

My father left the next day, moving some sixty miles away to pick apples at a large orchard. After a week, I drove to the orchard, where I found him picking apples from the top rung of a ladder leaning against the limb of a tree, his right arm in a sling. Looking up at him from beneath the ladder, I apologized and asked him to come home. He did return with me that afternoon, sitting next to me in the passenger seat of the 1956 Oldsmobile, with the red bandanna he wore while picking apples still wrapped around his head. Neither of us looked at the other or said a word during the entire sixty-mile return trip. I resumed my pattern of avoidance and left home for college, with academic and athletic scholarships, two years later.

My father and I had little to do with each other over the next twelve years, during which I fulfilled my own military obligation and completed my education. I had "war stories" of my own to tell by then and understood better what he had been revealing to me, as I was growing up, about the experience of war. He lived for only three years after our reconciliation, and died on August 2, 1981. I have never missed the turmoil, struggles, and estrangement between us, just him.

As I grew older and experienced the angst of life, my boyhood respect for my father returned. I realized that, in his own way, he had taught me to be the man I was and the man I was trying to become. He taught me about the importance of honesty and directness, with little tolerance for the bullshit of life; he taught me the honor of a man's handshake; he taught me how to fight, as men are sometimes required to do, with my fists. He taught me about competence, being good at whatever you do. He taught me about authority and power and the lack of it. He taught me how to be a father, even though his own example was often bad. He taught me how to lose, how to win, and how to walk away. He taught me of pain and the strength to struggle through it. He taught me the meaning of respect and the consequences of its absence. He taught me that sensitivity, caring, and compassion are often masked beneath pain, and about the symptoms that disguise it. And he showed me, literally and metaphorically, how to see the man in the moon!

I realized as a young man of thirty-two that my father was a compassionate and feeling man, trapped in the pain and anger of his own life struggles. He drank heavily to both numb and express the intensity of his feelings. And anger was not all he expressed while drunk or drinking. Despite the strife in the family, my father was someone to whom people in town turned for counsel, advice, and direction. I observed him often, as he sat at the bar in his favorite tavern, listening to the troubles and concerns of fellow patrons, providing them comfort, hope, reassurance, and understanding—a bar stool psychologist of sorts. He often sat quietly by himself, drinking coffee and smoking cigarettes at the kitchen table, with tears rolling down his face. I walked in on him once, so immersed in his agony that the cigarette he held in his unfeeling, crippled hand was burning the flesh of two fingers. I removed the cigarette from his hand, put it out in the ashtray, and left the kitchen with no recognition from him that I was there.

The late night and early morning of his death we talked about his tears and mine. He had idealized and worshipped me as a small boy, as much as I had worshipped him. Before I began school, he had taken me everywhere with him. I spent many an afternoon, sitting next to him on a bar stool, drinking orange pop and ginger ale while he sipped his beer. I was his "pride and joy," he said. He had bragged about me to his drinking buddies, about my prowess on the field and in the classroom. As I tried to become the man I thought he was not, we lost those feelings between us.

Once, I had been riding on his lap while he plowed a field with the old, borrowed Ford tractor. Attempting to finish the plowing ahead of darkness, he hit a large, unseen rock in the field. My head jerked forward and struck the steel lugnut that held the tractor's steering wheel to its shaft, gashing my head and right eyebrow. We sat in the front yard, the tractor left idle in the middle of the unfinished field; me still sitting on his lap and him holding the cold, ice cube-filled compress over my right eye. He said, "Look, the old man in the moon has come out."

"Where?"

"There, look. See, there's his nose."

I giggled at being able to see the old man in the moon, and fell asleep in my father's arms. "I'm gonna be like you, Dad, you know I'm gonna be like you." Of the scars I carry, the one above my right eyebrow is the most remembered and treasured.

In many ways, I am my father. Although I have never been a drinker or used drugs of any kind (other than cigarettes and coffee), and I have tempered and redirected my quickness to anger, I am nonetheless a sexist man in the ways my father taught me to be. I'm overly responsible and protective. I always walk on the outside with Janice, ready to "draw my sword" if necessary. I don't cry as much as I need to. Sometimes, I still withdraw into silence and attempt to hide the pain within. And, I still want at least fifty-one percent of the control in any relationship.

Although I have achieved a very privileged position in life as a tenured, full professor—whereas my father completed only the eighth grade and was a manual laborer his entire life—I am nevertheless a blue-collar academic and a stranger in paradise, fearing that someone in authority will see me as an imposter and force me to leave. But I think I am becoming the man my father had hoped I would become, actualizing the strengths and qualities he possessed but never realized. I believe these attributes have translated directly to my practice and teaching of therapy. My clients and students typically describe me as a tolerant, gentle, and compassionate man: wearing my feelings on my sleeve. And, in all honesty, I work best with blue-collar, working folks, first-generation college students, and people of color, because that is my experience and what I am familiar with. These are the people who are most attracted to my classes and practice of therapy. I have also continued to counsel Vietnam veterans over the years, and now their sons as well. Through it all, I am still more an idealist and dreamer than a realist, focusing more on what might be than what is.

I am passionately disturbed by the mistreatment of people (clients, students, or otherwise), and very much an advocate for the underdog, with a sense of fairness and justice always looming in the foreground. I sometimes have significant issues with authority figures, especially if I believe their incompetence or self-serving interests are harmful, or potentially harmful, to others or to me. At these times I often become confrontive, disarming people with my honesty, directness, and lower-class bluntness, believing it is better to be honest than kind.

My relationship with authority is a paradoxical one: I both fear it and respect it, the classic flight or fight response. On the fear side, I realize that those in positions of authority may use their power to exclude and otherwise severely harm me and others. If they exercise their authority in this manner, my initial response is to perceive them as incompetent and not worthy of my respect or loyalty. I then either avoid them or challenge them, based on my perception of the degree of harm being done to others or to me and the amount of their intrusion into our lives. If the intrusion is minimal, I avoid such authority figures. That is, I don't look for conflict with those in authority whom I perceive as incompetent and unworthy of my respect. However, if their intrusion and harm are perceived as significant, my response is to engage and challenge them. With regard to clients and students, if the intrusion and harm by those in authority is significant, I become their advocate and a source of support for students and clients: a buffer between them and authority. I typically become involved in a competitive win-lose engagement with authority figures, and I usually lose in some form or another because they have the power. Although I know what will happen, I nevertheless usually choose to engage in self-defeating conflict. With increasing experience, however, I am letting go more and more of this self-defeating behavior and learning the truth of Dickens's *Great Expectations:* people bring upon themselves their own comeuppance.

On the respect side of the equation, I support, attempt to please, and perceive as competent and worthy of my respect and loyalty those authority figures who respond to others and me with fairness, justice, and integrity. I am especially attracted to older men who exhibit these characteristics, perceiving them as a source of wisdom and mentoring—the father of my young boyhood and early thirties? With clients, students, and peers, I attempt to actualize and model these attributes of authority, mentoring, and wisdom, and, for the most part, I think I am successful in doing so.

On occasion, a professor of psychology emeritus drops by my office at the university to chat and see how I'm doing. His voice is gruff and his mannerisms often intimidating to others, but I look forward to his occasional visits and our talks with his inevitably sharing his wisdom with me and mentoring me in his own way.

Young men also seek me out. Following a recent guest lecture to undergraduate students, a young male student approached me and asked, "Are you a Vietnam veteran?"

"No, not a combat veteran. But I counseled combat veterans during Vietnam."

"I thought you knew about Vietnam. You have that same look in your eyes that my Dad did. My Dad was in Vietnam, but he would never talk to me about it. He died over the summer. Would you be willing to talk to me about Vietnam and my dad if I come to see you in your office?"

"I sure would. What's your name, son?"

I had made no mention of my involvement with Vietnam during my lecture that day, but this young man saw something in me that I would like to believe is a manifestation of what I have learned—and am still learning—about authority and therapy: respect, loyalty, fairness, justice, integrity, compassion, mentoring, and wisdom.

I talked with my son by telephone not long ago. He had just returned from Colorado, during his spring break from teaching. He said he was listening to the car radio as he drove through Nebraska, when the disc jockey played "Cat's in the Cradle." He said he began to cry at the song's beginning and continued for many miles after its ending.

> . . . Well he came from college just the other day
> So much like a man I had to say,
> "Son, I'm proud of you
> Can you sit for awhile?"
> . . . He'd grown up just like me
> My boy was just like me . . .
> "When you comin' home, son?"
> "I don't know when
> But we'll get together then, Dad, you know we'll have a good time then . . ."

But that's another story and, perhaps most appropriately, my son's to tell.

Chapter 8

The Vietnam Attachment

It's been twenty-eight years, almost half my lifetime, since I was honorably discharged from the United States Air Force. The concept seems an oxymoron to me: freed, liberated, released, excused, dismissed, exonerated, pardoned. My attachment to Vietnam is anything but discharged. Like many, I was too young—twenty-two—for the experience. Although I am not a combat veteran, my attachment to the men whom I counseled is still with me, an attachment from which I doubt I will ever be free. I have pushed bits and pieces deeply into my subconscious that still come to me when I go about my day, or in the midst of turbulent sleep. I remember Jamie, the militant African-American soldier who, his last day before being released from the hospital, gave me a braided bracelet made from boot laces and called me "brother." Billy B., whose right foot was finally amputated following a land-mine explosion in Vietnam and a half-dozen attempts by the surgeons to save it, comes to mind. I see the young quadriplegic man I befriended, whose name I cannot remember, dying of pneumonia as a result of the brain and spinal cord injuries he suffered in combat. There is Carl's disfigured face, without a mouth or nose. I recall our unit's commanding officer, a noncombat captain, who treated the soldiers as worthless failures because they had been physically or emotionally wounded.

Some of the bits and pieces I have talked about and shared with others, a select few—Janice primarily—but much larger pieces remain untold; I keep them to myself and from others, can't let themselves out even when I try. I share with other veterans of that war an attachment and bond that is most times unspoken—a glance, the posture of a stance, the startle at an unexpected noise, a wondering stare, a disconnection and intolerance for the trivial and trite, the acknowledgment of a stranger who looks familiar, a cracking wall in Washington D.C., a memorial to 58,191 lives that has become a place of healing for many, but not all.

I hang my American flags in their prominent places on the Fourth of July. The license plate on my car also displays an American flag, on a light-blue-and-white background: 853 VET, Connecticut Veteran. I cannot say why, these just seem the right things to do. More right than not standing for the national anthem or displaying any other kind of vanity license plates, such as "Preserve the Sound," "UCONN," or one of the catchy six-digit acronyms people put together for themselves. Mine is an attachment to a time, place, and people to whom I did not ask to be attached; it is a connection from which I cannot disconnect, though at times I would very much like to do so. It is a part of me, many times unwanted, indelibly etched into my life. Many times I feel this attachment as a burden and somberness, a seriousness and pensiveness, a loneliness and separateness.

My attachment began the year I was born, in 1946, after my father's return from World War II and four years of service to his country in the Netherlands, Belgium, France, and Germany and the battles of Normandy, Bastogne, Paris, and Berlin. My growing up years were filled with his stories of war, usually told while he was drunk and remembering the atrocities of combat. At first his stories were captivating and exciting. His buddies called him "Chief" because of his Chippewa (Ojibwa) lineage, and they all yelled, "Geronimo!" as they jumped from airplanes: he was a "Screaming Eagle." As I grew older, however, his stories—most times told in graphic detail—became more disturbing and frightening to me. My relationship with my father became fearful and insecure.

He told me of how he and his buddies left their American commanding officer lying wounded and dying in the snow of Bastogne rather than rescuing him, because he was a ninety-day wonder who knew nothing of combat and would otherwise get them all killed. He told me of the hanging of a German prisoner in an abandoned windmill in Holland. He would go repeatedly to the cedar chest in his bedroom to retrieve a handmade, bone-handled knife, telling me he had traded his bayonet with a German soldier in the woods of Belgium for the knife he held in his hand. He bragged of being called "Deadeye" by his fellow soldiers because he never shot a man unless he could shoot him in the head.

My attachment to my father also became entangled with my mother's relationship with him. I helped her hide his whiskey bottles or pour their contents down the drain of the kitchen sink. She and I would spend hours on Friday and Saturday evenings, sitting in the family's old 1941 Dodge parked on Main Street, waiting for him to emerge from the tavern so we could take him home. Every few hours, my mother would send me into the tavern to remind him that we were still waiting and to persuade him that it was time to leave. To my mother's frustration, I would usually end up on a bar stool drinking a ginger ale or orange pop as he retold to his drinking companions the stories that were already too familiar to me. On many occasions an argument would ensue, usually escalating to a physical fight between my father and one or more patrons of the bar. Even drunk, he was a feared pugilist in the town's local taverns, sending most of his combatants to the hospital. I witnessed many of these bar brawls as I increasingly became fearful of my father.

As I grew older, I stopped listening to my father's stories and avoided him through my academic and athletic activities in high school. At another level, though, I sought his approval and a more secure attachment to him. Although I never drank or used drugs, there was a time in my adolescence that I, too, became an antagonist, physically fighting with any male I could provoke or engage, including my father. I redirected this insecure, ambivalent, and resistant attachment to my father through a more socially acceptable form of physical expression by becoming a star athlete and football player in my small hometown. I translated my anger and aggression toward my father to the football field, where it was encouraged and valued. This athletic deftness serendipitously led to an athletic scholarship to college and a focus on academics rather than sports.

One event stands out brilliantly in my memory. It was Dads' Night during the football season of my junior year. My father had never attended any of my games, although I had secretly longed for him to do so. This night I wished he had not. I had already asked Coach to stand in as replacement for my father. Coach stood behind me in line as the players were introduced one by one over the loudspeaker, and their fathers walked from the sideline to stand behind them. I didn't know my father was at the game, sitting in the stands drunk. As my name was called, he staggered from his seat and walked to the edge of the field. As he approached the sideline, he tripped over the chain of the yard marker and fell on his face in the grass. Unable to stand by himself, he was helped to his feet by others, as people in the stands began chanting, mockingly, "Rollie, Rollie, Rollie." My father's name was Roland, but he was well known in town as Rollie, a drunk. My attempt to choke back tears was futile as I harshly wiped them from my face, smearing the shoeblack beneath my eyes. From behind, Coach leaned gently over my shoulder, firmly grasping my waist with his hands, and said, "Put your helmet on, Michael, he's still your father."

Defiantly, I turned and said, "Yeah, why don't you let him be your father tonight?"

He grabbed me by my shoulder pads and pulled me to his chest, holding me firmly in his grasp, and said, "How about you be my son tonight instead?"

I left home for college one season later, with football and academic scholarships. I injured my knee at the beginning of my sophomore year, ending my football career. In response, I went to college year-round, finished my bachelor's degree in three years, and began graduate school in the summer of 1968, eking out as much student deferment from the Vietnam draft as I could. But my time ran out. The Selective Service changed its status for graduate student deferments, and I received my induction notice in April 1969. My memory of the preinduction physical at Fort Wayne, in

Detroit, is still vivid, as is my last-minute decision not to accompany the other three young men who fled from Detroit to Canada instead of reboarding the bus. After all my father's stories, and his being a war hero and all, I just could not bring myself to run to Canada.

Not wanting to be an infantry soldier in Vietnam, I joined the United States Air Force under a delayed enlistment program, giving me time to finish the semester and my master's degree before entering basic training. I was inducted in Indianapolis on July 21, 1969, the day after the moon landing. I watched the landing on the TV in my motel room the night before I was sworn in and flown off to San Antonio, Texas, immobilized in a surrealistic fog of confusion, contradiction, and ambiguity. I sensed the bubbling belligerence and resistance within me, unsure and afraid, wishing it all would go away. Basic training was not all that difficult since I was in good physical condition and the military tests seemed easy after having spent four years in college. Eventually, I received orders for Denver, and a few months later began my assignment as a drug and alcohol counselor for returning Vietnam combat soldiers. The three years from May 1970 to July 1973 were the basis of my continued attachment to war, to the soldiers whom I counseled, and to my father.

In many ways, I was traumatized vicariously through my counseling of combat soldiers. Perhaps this occurred even earlier as a child, listening to my father's accounts of his war experience. I did not enlist in the military voluntarily, and I did not volunteer as a counselor for combat soldiers. Likewise, I did not choose my father and often wished for another, despite Coach's firm reminder that he was my father. Regardless, I became attached to my father and to the soldiers whom I counseled, to his and their stories, and to his and their lives and experiences, in combat and at home. Having no choice is both environmental and personal. I became their caregiver, responsive and available to hear about his and their losses, unresolved mourning, depression, traumas and atrocities, and repeated encounters with death. Although I was never in combat myself, I felt his and their situations through my personal involvement and emotional engagement with them.

Ironically, not all of these attachments are based on negative and traumatic experiences either, although many were. In the years following my discharge from the military, and in the later years of my father's life, before his death, my relationship with him became a secure and loving one. I believe my identifications and counteridentifications with him were evoked by the experiences of the Vietnam veterans I counseled, and my eventual loving connection to my father was the result of my work with these men. Like my father, they were combat veterans, and I was not. In addition, not only did the attachments with the men whom I counseled serve to bring my father and me together, my attachment to my father also helped me to form a caring and loving attachment and connection to them.

Some twenty-eight years later, I still read accounts and memoirs of Vietnam. (One of the best and most optimistic I have encountered recently is *The House of Purple Hearts,* by P. Solotaroff [Harper Collins 1995].) I have continued to encounter Vietnam veterans in need of counseling and, more recently, their sons and daughters as well. Although I am not as active as I once was in providing services to these soldiers, over the years I have volunteered my time and experience to veterans' groups and associations, exchanged counseling for cords of firewood with a veteran in northern Minnesota whom the Veterans Administration would not recognize as qualified for counseling, taught ex-soldiers whose children were born with birth defects from their fathers' exposure to Agent Orange, and talked with the children of Vietnam veterans who are estranged and confused by their parents' odd behavior, emotional distance, and lack of affection and attachment.

A memory comes to mind. While I was teaching overseas with Boston University in the late 1980s, it was the custom for the faculty and students to take a boat trip down the Nekar River the evening before graduation to watch the reenactment of the burning of the Heidelberg Castle. Sitting with a colleague in a small cafe that afternoon, I asked him if he was going on the boat ride down the river. He stared blankly into his drink and said, "I don't do boat rides." I asked him which rivers he had patrolled in Vietnam. He responded with a list of names. Still not looking up from his drink, he said, "I can't look at the deck of a boat without seeing blood." I nodded, lit a cigarette, and ordered two beers (even though I rarely drank). For the next couple of hours, he talked and I mostly listened. Although he didn't go on the boat ride, I did. But I couldn't look at the boat deck.

A picture of my father, dressed in his class-A army uniform, hangs on the parlor wall of our Victorian home in Connecticut, framed in walnut and the convex vintage glass of the 1940s. There are two additional pictures on the wall of my university office, one of which is my father receiving the silver star (with two oak leaf clusters) from General Maxwell Taylor after the Battle of the Bulge. The other is a collage, given to me by a former student and Vietnam combat veteran, of a kneeling soldier in combat dress with lowered head surrounded by the names of battles and firefights that occurred in Vietnam. On the back side of the picture—which I found years after he had given it to me—is his handwritten inscription: "I cannot bring you detachment's gift of casual reason; I've only my heart's emotion and deep, gentle sadness to give to you."

Chapter 9

I Took a Train Once

I was sitting in the back of the large auditorium, proofreading the final pages of my dissertation, when she walked in. I glanced up from the bonded, crisp white paper to examine the crowd. Her shoulder-length brown hair, with streaks of gray, wisped across the sides of her face as she walked toward an empty chair in the filled room. Her path would bring her within touching distance of my seat on the perpendicular aisle. She was the most striking, beautiful woman I had ever seen. My glance at the crowd was transformed into a fixated stare at this beautiful woman.

Our eyes met as she approached where I sat. I held a slender cigar in my mouth, a diminutive runlet of smoke drifting from its end. I had switched to cigars from cigarettes while writing the dissertation; they were cheaper and supposedly healthier because you didn't inhale—you could still smoke in public places in those days. As she walked directly in front of me, words formed in my haze-filled brain, as I gently rolled the tobacco leaf between my index finger and thumb. I said, "I took a train once, but they made me give it back." She smiled. Jesus, where did that comment come from, W. C. Fields for chrissakes? What must she think? Was that a dumb line, or what?

I was married to my high school sweetheart for seven years and had a three-year-old son. My wife was the only woman I had ever been with, sexually or otherwise, since the seventh grade. Why was I making stupid comments to a beautiful woman at a professional workshop where I was supposed to be one of the small-group leaders?

It was the spring of 1975, March, and I had been absorbed in my dissertation for months. What was the old adage, "In the springtime a young man's fancies turn to . . ."? No, it was just a fleeting remark, a smart-ass release from all the pressure and stress of finishing my doctorate. There must be two hundred people at the workshop and, chances are, I won't see her again in the next five days, I told myself. Let it go, there's no need to seek her out and apologize for your asinine comment.

The format of the workshop had participants attending a three-hour content presentation in the mornings, given by an expert on the topic of the day, then going to breakout groups in the afternoons to process the content of the morning's presentation. Ten doctoral students from the local university's department of counseling psychology—including me—were to facilitate the groups.

I continued to proofread my dissertation as the speaker rambled on about the therapeutic properties of some transcendent counseling intervention. The lecture ended, I marked my place in the unfinished editing, and checked the program agenda to find my assigned room. While the participants took a short coffee break, I arranged the chairs of my room in a circle, making sure I had a good view of each group member from the chair I had selected as my own. Then I walked out to the hallway to greet the members of my group, individually, as they found their way in the unfamiliar surroundings.

People were walking toward me, the coffee break over. There she was, among the crowd, checking the stenciled numbers above each doorway. Surely she would turn into one of the other rooms, soon, before she reached the place I was standing, with my heart throbbing and my palms sweating. Wrong! She walked to the entrance of my room, checked the number over the door again, smiled, said hello to me, and walked into the room. No smart-ass comment this time. I was stunned to silence.

I waited outside the room for a few stragglers to arrive and to breathe deeply and compose myself a little. We began the group by introducing ourselves briefly. She had a master's degree in clinical psychology and was the director of the juvenile division of a county probate court. She was also the highest-paid woman on the county's payroll, married to a successful businessman with three children, a son and two daughters. My breathing eased a bit. No harm, no foul, just a stupid one-liner by a stressed, sexist, doctoral student. We could both live with that. The remainder of the group membership was beige, except for Gwen, a young black Muslim from Wayne County, Detroit. Gwen expressed her dislike, hatred in fact, of white people as she introduced herself. Having been a student during the campus unrest of the mid to late 1960s, and having served in the military with young, militant black men during Vietnam, I figured I could at least avoid serious conflict with Gwen, even if I couldn't be facilitative with her.

But, the "I took a train once" lady remained a distraction to me. I left the group meetings immediately at the conclusion of each day: no time to socialize, putting the final touches on the dissertation, you know? I remained outwardly professional, detached, and objective—as I had been trained to do. Being a twenty-eight-year-old man socialized in the traditional gender roles of the times also made it easy for me to deny my feelings, rationalize, and stay focused on the group's objective. That same gender socialization, however, led me to appreciate the way her breasts filled the silk blouses she wore and to imagine how beautiful they must be, without the covering of silk. I mentioned my distraction and the obvious "countertransference" to my major advisor and the organizer of the conference workshop. He said something like, "Good, Mike, I thought you were going to graduate from this program without realizing you were human like the rest of us." What the hell did that mean? This wasn't helpful advice from my advisor, my mentor no less.

My group processed its way through the next few days. The cigars weren't appeasing me much. The beautiful woman observed me bumming cigarettes during breaks and asked what brand I smoked. She gave me a pack of my brand during our next time-out from processing, refusing to take any money in payment. It felt awkward but nice. It made me realize that no one had given me much of anything for a very long time, except my son. We talked briefly during a pause near the end of the workshop. I told her how happily married I was and showed her pictures of my son. She reciprocated by showing me pictures of her children, but she didn't mention being happily married.

The last day of the conference finally arrived. I had survived not only the test of my sexist gender role socialization, and the snare of countertransference; I had also received one of the highest group leader evaluations of the workshop. All that remained was to end the group. Since my Vietnam days, I had placed a great deal of emphasis on "saying goodbye" at the ending of things. Well, she ended things by reading to the entire group a poem she had written the night before our last group meeting, on a ragged edged piece of notebook paper torn from its wire spiral binding.

Four days earlier, at the beginning of the group, I had asked the members to introduce themselves by choosing an inanimate object that would help describe them to each other. As an example for the group, I had said that the inanimate object that would best describe me was, "snow on top of a mountain." That was the title of the poem—the one I mentioned earlier—she read to the group and then gave to me: Snow on Top of a Mountain.

She was not making this an easy goodbye. I didn't leave the workshop at the end of our final group session. She said she would like to talk for a while and I agreed. I briefly exchanged observations about our five days together with the other group members—including Gwen, who said she would probably like me if I weren't a white guy. Then Janice walked toward me from the parking lot, to where I stood on the sidewalk, after packing her luggage in her van. The conversation was superficial at first. We exchanged compliments about our participation in the group, her role as a member and mine as the leader. She said she would like to give me a hug before we parted. Her breasts felt as good against my chest as I imagined they would look naked, and she whispered in my ear that she didn't want to say goodbye yet.

We walked the grounds of the small Catholic college, greeting nuns who were strolling the tree-shaded sidewalks.

She slipped her hand into mine as we walked and gave it a gentle squeeze. I didn't object, although I was too absorbed in her assertiveness to respond and the moment of acknowledgment was gone. We continued to hold hands as we looked over the stone wall at the lazy ducks swimming in the pond below. She said how beautiful my teeth were, and before I could censor my response, I told her that the top, front ones weren't real; I had lost them in a fight with my dad at the age of fifteen. The honesty continued until dusk, with us sitting crossed-legged on a grassy knoll in the middle of the college campus.

We had grown up only thirty miles from one another, near Michigan State University. She was almost five years older than I and had been a high school cheerleader. I had been somewhat of a football star on my high school's team, playing in the same conference league as the high school team for which she had cheered. There weren't many opportunities for girls to participate in athletics in those days (1957 to 1960); cheerleading was the closest she could come to expressing her athleticism. Like me, she had married her high school sweetheart at the age of twenty and settled into the gender role expectations of our time—wife and mother. I was headed for a professorship at a small liberal arts college somewhere, and a house with a white picket fence. She was more ambivalent. There was a sense of restlessness and searching about her—she was "searching for a heart of gold"; that's what she said to me. The big house with the swimming pool, two expensive cars in the garage, and being a mother and wife weren't what they were promised to be.

We were both somehow different from our blue-collar, working-class upbringings—probably due to our education more than anything else. She was an alumna of Michigan

State and earned her master's degree in clinical psychology from Central Michigan. I was finishing my doctorate in counseling psychology at Western Michigan. When I asked her, she said the pewter dove pinned to a belt loop on her jeans was the symbol for NOW (National Organization of Women). I thought the pewter pin most likely explained her assertiveness and her differentness from other women I had met. But I also knew I was more than a little out of touch with contemporary women's issues. I had returned to Michigan from the military (a predominantly male experience for me) only two years earlier, and since that time I had been sheltered in graduate school. The only real feminist I knew was Gloria Steinem, and only from reading her books.

Our honesty became more intimate as we worked our way through the process of coming to know a stranger. Her husband had been physically abusive to her and she suspected affairs with other women. I hadn't been sexually intimate with my wife for almost two years, and I was beginning to question my sexual orientation and all those years in the boys' locker room with other men, although the coming and going of my erection as she and I talked was affirming my heterosexuality.

It was growing dark; we had extended the goodbye as long as we could. We both tried to put some finality to it, but we left it ragged and unfinished. Maybe we would have an opportunity to consult with each other, on a professional basis, some time in the future; we were, after all, both in the same field. I drove my Plymouth Duster the few miles home and told my wife about Janice, offering no excuses for my late return. The honesty of sitting on a grassy hill in the midst of the nuns at the small college, and talking with a woman who had been a stranger to me, was spilling over, and it felt good. I found out later that she had done the same with her husband.

The following Monday I returned to the university and my dissertation, trying to push her from my awareness. It was working until the phone rang a few days later. She wanted to see me; I said, "Yes, I would like to see you, too." I put my dissertation on the corner of my desk and worked on it only sporadically over the next few months. We met whenever we could, sometimes in a small-town park midway between the university and where she lived, sometimes at the university, once in a friend's apartment, and once in a motel. Before her, I had never talked as openly and honestly with anyone in my life, not a friend, not a family member, not my wife, and never with a client. But I had long ago crossed the professional line of counselor and client (group leader and member), pretending at times that we had become colleagues, and at other times feeling most like I was the client; especially the time she administered the Rorschach—ink blot—test to me. Although she gave me the test in the context of playfulness and fun, there was a seriousness to it as well. She was mistrustful of most men, and giving me the Rorschach was a way she could check me out a little more thoroughly; giving the Rorschach to clients was a routine part of what she did as a clinical psychologist. I had fallen in love with a strong-willed, assertive, strikingly beautiful, and extremely intelligent and sensitive feminist.

Our first night together at the friend's apartment was a lesson for me in what gender equality in a relationship between a woman and a man should be. Her breasts were more beautiful than I could ever have imagined, but we would not have intercourse that night. Maybe it was my guilt about adultery, or my awkwardness in having been with only one other woman in my life, or maybe I wasn't the typical sexist man I thought I was, but intercourse was out of the question. She calmly said, "It's okay, roll over and I'll rub your back." Later, we sat naked on the concrete patio, wrapped together in a blanket, under the overhang of the porch roof, as a thunderstorm rumbled around us and she sipped a milkshake that I had gotten for her upset stomach from the nearby Diary Queen. We fell asleep on the couch, wrapped around each other's nakedness. I awoke early the next morning and made the final revisions to my dissertation while she slept on the couch.

She left her husband on July 4, met me in my hometown, and I took her to my parents house to meet them. Mom was visibly shaken when I introduced Janice to her, told her that my marriage had not been going well for a long, long time, and that I was in love with Janice. But Mom already knew my marriage wasn't going well. It was just the shock of meeting Janice with no warning and all the information coming at her at one time that threw her off balance. But she recovered quickly, and she and Janice got to know one another better as they talked and prepared supper together in the kitchen. Rollie's response to Janice was different from Mom's initial distress. Rollie liked her immediately. But then, he never liked my wife much; in truth, he actively disliked, maybe hated, her. She was outwardly demeaning to him, perceived him as less than she, and talked down to him. To her he was a drunk and a negative influence on our son, not worthy to spend time with him. But she treated Rollie poorly even before our son was born. We rarely visited my parents because "he's always drunk," she said. He was sometimes drunk when we visited him, but not always. To my wife, having one drink of whiskey defined being drunk.

Janice's response to Rollie was different, too. Rollie had built a small cinderblock sun porch—with lots of ceiling-to-floor windows—on the east end of our old house. He loved to sit in the sunporch in summer afternoons and evenings and watch television. It was cooler, brighter, and felt more open, he said. He and Janice were talking together when I walked into the room after spending time with Mom in the kitchen. He was sitting in his big overstuffed leather chair, and Janice was sitting on the floor in front of him. She was asking him about his life and his time in World War II. She had been a history teacher for five years before becoming a clinical psychologist and had some knowledge about Rollie's war experience, which was endearing to him. But what was amazing to me was that Rollie was answering her questions openly and honestly, not only about the war but about his life as well. He had his share of questions for her, too, and she reciprocated with openness and honesty. I sat on the couch and listened quietly. They liked each other immediately. After they had talked together for a long while Rollie looked at Janice's chest and said, "You look like Dolly Parton." I thought to myself, "Oh, boy, here we go. She's going to rip his testicles off for that comment."

Instead, she looked at Rollie in the eyes and said, "Well, thank you. I'm glad you think I'm attractive."

Rollie held her stare and smiled, "You're welcome." Rollie and Janice were alike in many ways. Both were forthright, direct, cut through the bullshit of ordinary social conversation, and checked people out with their blunt, teasing, and sometimes caustic, stinging, and offensive comments to them. Despite their strongly held beliefs and attitudes about some things, they were also very accepting of differing points of view if people were straightforward with them.

I received my doctorate a little more than a month later, in August, still living with my wife. I didn't know Janice was standing among the fieldhouse crowd during graduation, outside the area designated for friends and family. She moved to the edge of the processional exit to touch my gowned arm, tears in her eyes, and then disappeared into the mass of bodies. Tears filled my eyes as I ran from the fieldhouse to find her, but she was gone. I will always remember her coming to my graduation and touching my arm: her way of acknowledging how important the accomplishment was to me, her way of giving to another despite the discomfort to her, her sensitive and knowing way of saying, "I love you," with a mere touch.

The next several months were difficult, to say the least. In early September, I left my wife and took a position at a small liberal arts college in northeastern Ohio. Janice was accepted to the doctoral program in counseling psychology at Kent State University, and we were making plans to live together. Then one Saturday morning in late September, my wife arrived in the driveway of my college-provided house—accompanied by a U-haul truck driven by one of her friends and loaded with all her belongings. I was adamant about wanting out of the marriage and continuing my relationship with Janice. This made little difference to my wife; she was staying, she said, and she unloaded the rental truck. Although Janice and I saw each other regularly, it was April of the following year before I showed up at her apartment in Kent where she had begun her graduate course work. It was late, almost midnight, when I knocked on her door and she answered. "Do you still want a roommate?" I asked.

She began to cry. "Yes," she said, and then embraced me and whispered in my ear, "I never thought it would happen."

Our twenty-six-year love story has taught me much about myself and my relationships with others. I think women know more about things related to gender than men do. As a man I have often felt stuck in the sexist biology of my genes. I'm overprotective sometimes, still believing it's my role and responsibility, solely, to protect and provide. I still get angry before I can touch the pain and fear that underlie the protective defensiveness of my anger. At other times, I think it's my place to take control of an unruly situation before it gets out of hand or to insure that things get done. I still believe men are physically stronger than women and that men should position themselves on the outside when walking with a woman. These are silly things perhaps, but they are vestiges of my gender role sexism that may have been ingrained through socialization or embedded in my Y chromosome.

I have learned the consequences of nonconformity to traditional gender role expectations, even though present-day relativists and reconstructionists likely would argue that traditional gender roles no longer exist. Nonetheless, the court-appointed psychologist and judge said I was too much a friend to my son, not enough a father figure, and custody of my son was awarded to my wife during the divorce proceedings and custody battle—a mêlée I have long regretted. Janice did not get custody of her three children either. "You're more concerned with your career than being a mother," the judge said. "Besides, you have been unfaithful in your marriage, and you are not willing to admit your extramarital affair was a one-night stand and return to your husband to reconcile the marriage."

Janice received her Ph.D. in 1978 from Kent State, after which I took a new faculty position and she accompanied me to Iowa. It was a place of made-right hamburgers and "A

Place to Grow," a double entendre painted on the roadside sign at the Illinois state line—which referred mostly to growing corn, but it conveyed an existential meaning as well. Janice wrote her dissertation and studied for her comprehensive examinations in the small bedroom of our rented townhouse, with time left over for an administrative internship with the dean of the college. We were offered a two-for-one position at Northern Iowa: one position and one salary split between the two of us. We declined and I followed Janice to the University of Minnesota-Duluth, where we taught members of the Chippewa Tribe in the Native American Indian Alcohol and Substance Abuse Counselor Training Project. The grant supporting the project expired four and one-half years later, and I took a position in January at Tulsa University. Janice stayed in Duluth. Tulsa was a place of jacked-up, big-wheeled, four-wheel-drive pickup trucks with rifles hanging from gun racks in their rear windows and all the prejudiced attitudes that accompany the trucks' description. Shortly after I moved to Oklahoma, Janice left Minnesota and went to Syracuse University as an assistant professor.

Tulsa University recruited her away from Syracuse in an attempt to keep me there, at a smaller salary than mine and less than what she was receiving at Syracuse. The dean told her, "The difference in your salary should be worth it to sleep with your husband." Then there was the dildo that a male faculty member placed in her hand at their first meeting. It was just a good ol' boy, Oklahoma way of greeting the new female faculty member. But the Southwest Sunbelt wasn't prepared for an assertive, associate professor feminist from the Midwest or the likes of Germaine Greer, who taught at

Tulsa for a while and labeled it "the banana belt republic" when she left after just one year.

Without providing the gory details, suffice it to say there were many sexist issues and gender role conflicts. As a result, several academic programs were dissolved at the university, and with the dissolution, the faculty positions of two untenured associate professors were also dissolved.

Those were difficult times for Janice and me, and at times we thought the gender role conflicts in our relationship would destroy the love story. We fought about our differences, based almost entirely on gender. It became so extreme that we once argued over whether a woman could urinate as far as a man, based on my angry rebuttal to her during the argument: "Go piss up a rope." We argued about whose turn it was to follow whom to the next faculty position, who made the most money, whose career was more important, who had been most affected by gender oppression and sexism (I always pulled out the Vietnam thing), what role sex played in defining a man's identity and its place in an egalitarian relationship, ad infinitum. There seemed to be no resolution to our gender differences.

A good friend arranged a one-year distinguished visiting scholar position for me at Temple University, just as my unemployment benefits ran out. Again Janice followed me, this time to Philadelphia and a rented row house on Fairmont Avenue, near the old, abandoned prison and the Art Museum. She worked with the athletic teams at Temple, adjuncted in the counseling psychology department, and taught part-time at the City College of Philadelphia. The one-year position at Temple ended, and Janice was offered a position in the counseling center at Washington State, working with the athletic teams there. I followed her to the rolling hills of the Palouse and its wheat fields. I became a househusband and began writing my still unfinished novel.

The unplanned gender role reversals were helpful to understanding the difficulties of each other's position. But my gender role socialization and the Y chromosome kicked in again, and I began to feel inadequate without a job and a financial burden to Janice. I was offered a teaching position with Boston University's Overseas Programs and left for Germany one year after moving to Pullman, Washington, in the fall of 1987. Janice remained at Washington State. *Ausfart Amerika!*

My first teaching assignment was in Berlin, West Germany. For a man who felt out of step with what was expected of him in his own country, I fell in love again, this time with Europe. I rekindled the romanticism—albeit sexist—that was buried somewhere inside me. There was emptiness in the absence of that strikingly beautiful woman I had told about the train I once took but had to give back. I asked Janice to visit me in Germany and let her know of my planned attempt to seduce her to Europe, to be with me. I took the overnight military duty train from Berlin to Frankfurt—West Berlin was an island city in the midst of surrounding Eastern bloc Communist countries, still monitored by the allies of World War II: France, Britain, the Soviet Union, and the United States. The duty train was the easier of two ways to travel by land from West Berlin, through East Germany to West Germany, the other being to travel by automobile, with strict time lines to complete the designated route, Soviet checkpoints, searches, and harassing paperwork. When the duty train arrived at the station the following morning, I caught the *U-bahn* from the *bahnhof* to the airport in Frankfurt, to meet Janice's flight from Seattle. We made love in our private train compartment and slept naked on the duty train back to Berlin that night. We lived in Germany for three years, and I fell in love with her all over again. She fell in love with me again, too, and with Europe.

We are beginning our twelfth year at the University of Connecticut. She's the director of the alcohol and substance abuse prevention program at the university, and I am a faculty member in the counseling psychology program. We're still teaching, living, and modeling the lessons we have learned from our twenty-six-years together. After all my years as a therapist and an educator of therapists, I continue to find the relationships between members of a couple to be the most common issue in counseling.

Most times I think Janice and I are helping our students and clients move toward gender equality in their intimate relationships, but I often wonder. Unlike twenty-six years ago, there are now sexual harassment legislation and policies, laws, and rules that prohibit and punish gender role and sexual orientation discrimination, and "blue lighted" (emergency phones designated by blue lights) campuses to remind women of the possibility of rape. In many ways, though, the same gender issues are prevalent today as twenty-six years ago, despite the development of laws that attempt to govern our behaviors. In many respects, and sadly, the more recent legislation and policies have also provided the vehicles for some people to get even or avenge the injustices and transgressions of past and present gender bias, rather than providing the tools for gender resolution and reconciliation.

Many times I am not sure what to do with, or how to respond to, the hostility of many new age feminists toward men. These feminists are very different from the beautiful, feminist woman I met at a conference in 1975, with her pewter dove pinned to the belt loop of her jeans. To me the current feminists are academic, theoretical, and seem to be seeking—demanding—entitlement and special privileges more than gender equality. When I bought a new pickup truck (not the Oklahoma kind, but a very conservative, gray, four-wheel-drive, mid-sized Nissan truck)—merely a practical choice for the Connecticut winters—a female student noticed the new vehicle and said, "Well, I guess driving a truck makes you a 'real man.'" I replied, "I wish you had told me that earlier; I could have saved myself a hell of a lot of work over the years." Or the young woman who observed me hugging a male student in the hallway of the education building, and commented sarcastically, "Oh, I just love to see men 'bonding.'" I responded by saying, "I always think of bonding as some type of metallurgic, chemical reaction, not how people relate to one another." I realize these are not the best responses to foster gender resolution, but I am not beyond becoming defensive to sexist comments made to me or immune to being lumped into a jaundiced feminist perspective of men. Many of these women were born in the early to mid-1970s—some even later—and have little historical sense of the women's movement and its initial goals and agendas.

I have found that I cannot counsel some women (or men for that matter), and make the appropriate referrals, usually to a female therapist in the case of women clients. Maybe these women are too similar to my former wife. Maybe they are too constricted in their view of themselves; too self-limiting in the choices, options, and responsibilities necessary for them to attain the things they want in life; too angry, too narrow in their perceptions of expected and possible gender roles; too narrow in their vision of the way relationships and the world should be rather than are. In my mind, resolving gender role conflicts is a process, not an event. I believe dogmatic people work best with other, like-minded dogmatic people. I believe the same holds true in therapy; dogmatic therapists work best with dogmatic clients.

Moreover I'm not sure what the word feminist means any longer; it has taken on so many connotations over the years. I do know, though, that I need to nurture and validate those who are seeking their identity, gender and otherwise. I've learned that people must first discover who they are and where they're going before they decide whom they want to be with. I have learned that I don't have to go along with them to understand their journey. I can understand from my own experiences and knowing myself, from living gender role differences and conflicts (consciously anyway) for twenty-six years and learning from the woman I love and our relationship. I have learned that rigidly conceived yet accepted interventions in therapy, as well as politically correct gender role legislation, laws, and policies, should not kill an emotionally intimate, loving, longing, sensual, and sexual relationship between a woman and a man.

I'm not a pseudoliberated man of the nineties and the new millennium. I don't go into the woods with other men to beat on a drum and read poetry aloud to find my identity as a man. I've had a fire in my belly for as long as I can remember. But then, I never went into the woods to hunt animals or catch fish as a way of defining my manhood, either. I don't consider myself soft, but neither am I callous or insensitive. I served my country during Vietnam. I've had a job since I was sixteen years old, and I still believe an honest day's pay deserves an honest day's work. I've never believed I was entitled to anything but, rather, that I had to demonstrate that I was deserving of an opportunity or privilege. Perhaps this is an easier thing for a perceived white man to believe and say—I easily passed for white and rarely disclosed my mixed-blood Ojibwa heritage. But such an attitude also may depend on who the man is, where he has come from, how he got to where he is, and whom he has become. I'm still sexist in many ways. The powerful gender role socializations can never be totally erased. More important, though, my sexism doesn't oppress others. I've always been an advocate for the underdog. As the saying goes, "It takes one to know one," and to know the underdog's need for an advocate.

I am my father in many ways: lower class and blue collar. In my younger years, I was too easy to anger and too quick to fight, with a bit of a chip on my shoulder and a feeling of inadequacy about my place. But I am somehow different from my father: different life experiences in a different time and in different places with different people. Some things I learned from my father I brought with me, other things I discarded and replaced with my own. Ironically though, most of what I have learned about being a man has come from my relationship with a woman—that strikingly beautiful woman. I have come to believe that it is through relationships that one learns about one's gender roles and biases. I have come to believe that clients and students (female as well as male) can learn about their gender roles, their conflicts, their biases, their choices, and their potential through a relationship in an educational and therapeutic context, with a man who is a little out of step and still in the process of defining himself—with all his limitations and flaws. Sometimes we find what we want by discovering what we don't want.

Maybe it's because of Connecticut, "the land of steady habits," that I have the feeling that old attitudes about gender roles and their accompanying expectations are generally slow to change. I think it's more than Connecticut attitudes, though; the attitudes are pervasive and widespread. In some ways they're similar to the orbit of a comet and the notion of iteration in chaos theory. What goes around comes around. But like the repeating, iterating, recycling pattern of an orbiting comet, old ways of thinking reappear in their life cycle, except that no matter how close they come to resuming their earlier course of travel, they never take the same exact path.

As for the strikingly beautiful woman—her shoulder-length brown hair with streaks of gray wisped across the sides of her face—to whom, in 1975, I said, "I took a train once. . ."? She is, beyond doubt, the most talented and gifted therapist and educator I have ever known or observed practice and teach. Beyond that, we are partners in what I consider to be the closest any couple could come to an egalitarian relationship. Due, I believe, to *her* ability to transcend gender roles, to understand both men's and women's gender differences and conflicts, and to continue to hold and gently squeeze the same hand that she slipped hers into and caressed twenty-six years ago.

She once said to me, while we were teaching and living in Germany—maybe it was during our first time taking the duty train from Frankfurt to West Berlin, lying together naked after making love, listening to the clacking of the rails beneath us, watching the flashes of light that entered our compartment from the hazy glow of small European village street lamps as we passed them—"I have always loved trains."

Chapter 10

Racehorse in the Barn

Blaze and the sorrel mare stretched their necks through the open top half of the split door, banging their chests against the weathered boards of the closed bottom half, as I approached the cinderblock barn that served as their stable. This image has stuck in my memory since I was five. Seeing me approach their livery, the two horses, in anticipation of their release, labored, pounded, and pranced to be free of the confines of the barn.

Blaze was my sister's horse. He was large, beautiful, and chocolate-colored with an entirely white face. I never knew the mare's name; she was always referred to merely as "the mare," and was my father's horse. Blaze was the gentle one of the two, despite his larger size. He was purely a riding horse, with a speed reflective of his name. My sister would place me in front of her on Blaze's saddle, so I could get a good grip on the saddle horn, and we would storm off to the nearby pasture where Blaze would run and run, with no notice of the two of us on his back. The mare, on the other hand, was a quarter horse and in her younger years had cut cattle on a farm and occasionally worked a rodeo. She was wonderful to watch as my father raced her up and down the gravel road near our house. While charging full speed in one direction, with the flick of a rein, she would dig her rear hooves into the gravel, looking as if she were going to sit on her haunches, spin in a one-hundred-eighty-degree turn, and charge off in the direction from which she just came. With a slightly different movement of the rein, when my father removed one foot from the stirrups, the mare would again dig in her back hooves, come to a complete stop, and begin to back-step as my father dismounted her. I would sit on the back porch for hours and watch my father "work" the mare. I eternally protested the horses' return to the barn. It seemed unnatural to me that such beautifully free and powerful animals should be restrained in a stall.

I have always loved horses, although both Blaze and the mare left my life by the time I was seven. Blaze was bought by a local farmer, for his children to ride, when my sister left home at sixteen. Shortly after Blaze left, Dad sold the mare to a man employed by the railroad. She continued as a working horse, walking the railroad lines as her rider checked the rails for damaged ties and loose spikes. Some ten years after the horses were sold, I would drive after school to the homestead of the farmer who bought Blaze, park my 1956 Oldsmobile next to the fence that surrounded the farmer's pasture, and watch Blaze frolic and trot free in the open fields, free of any riders and constraints in his older years.

In the years since, I have continued to love horses and all that they once represented, and continue to represent, to me. For much of my life, I have felt I had something in common with Blaze and the mare: I felt like a racehorse in a barn. I felt as if my potential would never be truly actualized. External forces imposed constraints beyond my control, and there was always someone to say, "no," rather than, "give it a run." As a small boy, I couldn't reach the latch to the barn door, so I couldn't free the horses from their confinement. As I grew older, the door latch to my own freedom was controlled by others. Like Blaze and the mare, when freedom presented itself, I ran and ran. Along the way, and still today, others would return me to the barn, deciding when and if I might be free again to run at my own pace and for as long as I wished. All the potential, all the strength and beauty, all the love of life and freedom, all the playfulness—restrained. And sometimes, when long races have been lost or a trauma has brought me up lame, I have returned to the barn of my own volition and remained there for a while, languid and hesitant to bolt again. Nonetheless, the passion always returns and grows stronger, there are races to run, work to do, and ranges to caper across.

When I am unable to fully grasp something I am trying to describe or understand, I often resort to metaphors to explain the inexplicable. The Greek interpretation of metaphor means to transfer the quality of one entity to another. Thus, I use metaphors to link one idea to another, which, in some cases, is not merely descriptive but also transformative. It is this descriptive and transformative use of metaphors, and their reorganizational power, that has sustained and promoted growth for my clients, and for myself as a therapist.

As a therapist, I perceive individuals as fluid, nonlinear, dynamical, self-organizing, and in a continuous process of emerging. More important, I characterize individuals in terms of their narratives, which include storytelling and creating and recreating themselves. The metaphors of pathologies, diagnoses, and conceptualizations that describe clients by their psychological deficits are not appropriate for me. Rather, I see the overall patterns of life as a continuous story in which we are all capable of replacing problem stories and psychological labels with alternative and more viable narratives and descriptions. In other words, for me, there are no pathologies, only stories that have gone awry. I thus emphasize the complexity and "multivoicedness" that emerge from my clients' narratives. This also means that each individual's story is completely independent and different from the story told by another, and clients' metaphors are a way of giving meaning to life experiences and seeking comprehension.

I first met Edil on a military post while I was teaching overseas for Boston University. He was a master's degree student in counseling psychology and had joined the United States Army some eight years earlier, to expand his options in life. Edil had grown up in the public housing projects of Puerto Rico, excelling as a golden-glove boxer. His biggest dream had been to earn a position on the United States Olympic boxing team. He had lost his dream, by a close judges' decision, in the final bout that determined selection to the Olympic team. Following his defeat, he had turned to academics as a new dream (and his mother's dream for him): to earn a Ph.D. in psychology.

I learned all of this in my role as Edil's clinical-practice supervisor for his master's program. Although verbally proficient in English as a second language, despite his strong Spanish accent, Edil struggled with written English—which negatively affected his academic performance, his confidence, and his ability to attain his dream of a Ph.D.

Listening to his boxing stories and his confident self-referent metaphors to boxing, I began to pick up on and use these metaphors in my work with Edil. He described himself, metaphorically, as "a puncher, never giving up, a fighter, tough and durable, capable of taking a blow and getting up from the mat, learning form his mistakes, being 'coachable,' and able to accept defeat."

Such self-referent metaphors characteristically guide my use of metaphors with clients and are reflected in the approach I take with them. I began assigning academic meaning to Edil's boxing metaphors and stories, believing that his present, personal story consisted of these past meaningful events, and that they were likewise applicable from a future perspective. I further believe client's personal stories, such as Edil's, are multidimensional, permitting people to adapt numerous spatiotemporal vantage points (past, present, and future) when telling their stories.

Gradually, Edil began to gain confidence and belief in his present and future academic and writing abilities, based on the confident and successful metaphors of an accomplished boxer. I returned to the United States from Europe before Edil, three years after our first meeting. A year later, he was assigned from Germany to West Point, a three-hour drive from the University of Connecticut, where I was teaching. Edil was accepted to Connecticut's Ph.D. program in counseling psychology for the following fall semester. He draped a pair of miniature boxing gloves over the rearview mirror of his car as he commuted from West Point to Connecticut for classes. He resigned from the Army the next year, pursued his Ph.D. studies full-time as a graduate assistant, and graduated with a doctorate in psychology in 1995. He is now a tenured associate professor at the University of Nevada—and still a "fighter" with a dream.

A segment of the acknowledgements section of Edil's dissertation reads as follows: *"This dissertation is the culmination of a long journey that began with a dream of becoming a more acceptable helper, a liaison for social change, and an equalizer for the people of the public housing projects on my beloved island of Puerto Rico."*

Of great personal significance to me is the first line of his dissertation's dedication, in Spanish: *"Me gustaria dedicarle este humilde trabajo a las personas más importantes en mi vida; al maestro (Dr. Michael P. Wilbur), sin su paciencia y amor nunca lo hubiera logrado"*; and a handwritten note on the inside cover: *"To El Maestro, Thanks for being there when I was alone. With love to Dr. Mike, Edil."*

Using the stories people tell to me (a narrative approach), I have also come to realize that I need to be comfortable with a certain degree of confusion and dissonance in the therapeutic process, as my clients and I assign different meanings and comprehension to their metaphors and stories. Similarly, I have found clients who are more inclined to explore existential issues, to probe life problems in more profound ways, and to tolerate the ambiguities of reorganizational processes in such metaphorical, meaning-making ways benefit most from my narrative approach to therapy.

A client experiencing severe depression recently began our session with, *"I feel totally overwhelmed, like I'm in a sinking boat. And no matter how fast I bail the water, I keep sinking deeper and deeper. There are all these distractions, and I feel like I'm going in a hundred different directions at once. I don't care any longer, let it sink."*

In brief, her story is that of a single parent raising three children, working full-time, and attending college in the evenings—with all the stress and responsibilities that such a life situation entails. I asked her if she could see land from her position in the sinking boat. She looked confused, so I repeated my question. She smiled and said, "Yeah, I guess, I guess I can see land."

"Then why don't you just sail the boat toward land, rather than bailing water? Just keep sailing the boat and you may reach land before it sinks."

A grin began to wrinkle the corners of her mouth.

"Have you ever sailed before?" I asked.

"No."

"Well, usually a boat is sailed in a zig-zag direction, rather than in a straight line. But, in your situation, I think it would be better if you just sailed the boat directly toward land. No bailing and no zig-zagging."

At our next session, in response to my query about how she was doing, she said with a smirk, "Much, much better thank you. Just sailing the boat."

I should also note that I don't know what metaphors will resonate with my clients and be helpful in promoting their growth. For example, different metaphors have different assumptions about how to live life within that particular metaphor, and I have found no singular metaphor that captures all the complexity of life or the essence of human passion. Regardless, I value the use of metaphors in therapy and realize their impact in restructuring and reorganizing the meaning of individual stories, life-events, and histories that have gone amiss.

From this narrative perspective, I have been able to maintain a passionate interest in the work I do and in the people with whom I spend time. When it comes to me, I am especially fond of the metaphor of the racehorse in the barn. This metaphor has helped me to reframe life events and experiences, permitting new meanings to emerge for thoughts, feelings, and behaviors that have become "stuck" in their iterating cycles. The use of this metaphor and others in my own life has also helped me to discover and use metaphors that help my clients develop new meanings for and insights into their often entangled and snarled problems.

As for my own story, I have learned that the countryside is strewn with barns, some built by others and some of my own making. I have learned that with metaphors I am capable of replacing my problem stories with more viable stories and descriptions of my life-events, feelings, thoughts, and behaviors. I have been able to transform and reorganize discouragement and despair into renewed passion, interest, and hopefulness.

While in the military, one of my favorite songs was "A Horse with No Name" by America. This song seemed to tell my story and that of my clients' at the time, "I've been through the desert on a horse with no name, it felt good to be out of the rain . . ." Given the social, cultural, and political context of that era, and my own social and political ideology, I also identified with a particular movie of the time, *They Shoot Horses, Don't They?*

I was in a barn of someone else's making, I did not choose to be there, I wanted my freedom, I could not endure my four-year confinement and constraint, I could not tolerate the control and power others held over me, I could not bear the emotional and physical pain suffered by those I was counseling (and that I had suffered as well). Why didn't "they" just shoot us all and put us out of our misery: "They shoot horses, don't they?" My borrowed metaphors and personal story became cynical, negative, pessimistic, hopeless, and self-defeating. I lost passion for therapy and the people I was counseling.

My negativity transferred to my clients, and I became ineffective. I lost control of a therapy group and the members turned on me, physically. I spent a week in the same hospital in which I worked as a therapist with four broken ribs. I recovered from the fractured bones and returned to the therapy group and the men who had hospitalized me. I gained excessive weight and then lost it in a short time. I was again hospitalized and misdiagnosed (I discovered five years later) with a serious illness.

During my second hospitalization, I spent time each day in physical rehabilitation, along with soldiers who were amputees or who had suffered severe brain trauma and spinal cord injuries in Vietnam. I befriended a young, quadriplegic man, wheeling him to and from therapy each day and talking with him for hours. On one particular day, his catheter bag had become full of urine and overflowed on the physical therapy room floor just as we approached the sign-in desk. A butter bar, what we enlisted men called a second lieutenant due to the tan color of the bar they wore on their shoulder, at the desk became enraged at the puddle on the floor and began screaming at the young man in the wheelchair to clean up his "fucking mess." Tears began to stream down the young man's face as he stared at the pool of urine on the floor. With disrespect, I looked the lieutenant square in the eyes and said to him, "That's okay, sir, I got it. What's a little piss between friends; but what would you know about friends?"

My metaphors and personal story began to change after this experience. Yes, I was confined to someone else's barn, but I was still a racehorse: capable of actualizing my potential, with none of the limitations of being in a wheelchair. The young, quadriplegic man died a few weeks later from respiratory complications of pneumonia. I always said he died from Vietnam, not pneumonia. Nevertheless, I returned to my duties as a therapist shortly after his death. I engaged my clients with a passion for therapy and an emotional intimacy that I had never experienced before. I was a racehorse again, freed from the barn of my own making. In 1973, I was awarded Outstanding Airman of the Year for my work with my fellow soldiers. The name of the young soldier I befriended is on "the wall" in Washington D.C., although I have never gone there to see it. But I will go one day to thank him again, and to thank the other soldiers I counseled, for changing my metaphors and transforming my life-story.

I found a new metaphor not long ago in *The Horse Whisperer* (1995) by Nicholas Evans. It's yet another to add to those I have accumulated and used over the years to stay alive and grow in my profession. The gist of the metaphor is a horse traumatized by a dire collision with a tractor-trailer truck during a winter ride, confined afterward to a darkened barn and abandoned for fear of his aftermath violence.

The Horse Whisperer: "It's always kind of interesting to hear the horse's side of the story. . . . It's all about self-preservation. . . . You see, these animals have got such big hearts, there's nothing they want more than to do what you want them to. But, when they get confused, all they can do is try to save themselves" (Evans 1995, 103, 105).

By listening and whispering to the horse, the whisperer changed a story that had gone awry, from one of confusion, self-preservation, and violence to living life with an impassioned, big heart.

This metaphor has particular appeal to me because I have been both the horse and the whisperer during the course of my professional life. At times of confusion, pain, and despair, it has taken all I could do to stay in the profession and continue the work I do, despite the largeness of my heart and the passion for what I do. I have experienced trauma and darkened barns. And sometimes I have acted like an old fire horse, my reactions stronger than my common sense. Another person listening to my side of the story and gently whispering has helped me to change my confused, indifferent, and self-preserving narratives to a story of strength, beauty, playfulness, hope, renewed commitment, and ardor for life and what I do.

I live mostly in an academic barn these days, with many external constraints, conditions, stipulations, controls, and restraints: administrative micromanagement, a consumer and business mentality rather than an academic one, labor relations and collective bargaining, publish-or-perish pressure, faculty politics and hidden agendas, and minds of a common quantitative bent. Still, I maintain my passion for what I do and the people with whom I work when I am out of the barn—doing therapy and in the classroom. This is where I run free and unrestricted, listening, whispering, and helping to create and recreate life stories with my metaphors and narratives. In the true spirit of a racehorse: "Away with the cant of 'Measures not men'!—the idle supposition that it is the harness and not the horses that draw the chariot along. If the comparison must be made, if the distinction must be taken, men are everything, measures comparatively nothing" (George Canning, speech to House of Commons [1802]).

In my position as a therapist and teacher,

Now the great winds shoreward blow;
Now the salt tides seaward flow;
Now the wild white horses play,
Champ and chaf and toss in the spray.
— Matthew Arnold, "The Forsaken Merman" (1849)

It is the language of metaphors, my ability to whisper new stories into stories that have gone astray, and my belief in my potential to positively influence lives that sustain my passion for my work and the people I counsel and teach. And knowing there will always be barns and racehorses wanting to run free.

Chapter 11

Mavericks, Renegades, and Other "Cowboy" Therapists

My family didn't get its first television until 1956, when I was about ten years old. Before that, a couple of my boyhood buddies and I would sneak after dark to the house of an old man who lived in one of the wealthier parts of town. We would lie on a grassy knoll by the giant maple tree in his yard and watch his television through his large picture window. It didn't matter that we couldn't hear the sound, except occasionally through an open screen door or window; the images were enough!

With fascination, we watched the Lone Ranger, Wild Bill Hickock, Gabby Hays, Roy Rogers, Gene Autry, The Cisco Kid, Lash Larrou, Hop-Along-Cassidy, *Gunsmoke*, and *Maverick*. As a young boy, like others my age, I wanted to be a cowboy when I grew up. A "good" cowboy, one of the "white hats," not one of the "bad guys" who always wore the "black hats." At that early age, I was drawn, I believe, to the prevalent themes of those early television Westerns: good triumphing over evil; justice prevailing; the underdog overcoming impossible odds; the freedom of riding Silver, Trigger, or Champion through the open desert and plains; the absence of law and order (rules) in the "Wild Wild West"; the reliance on oneself and rugged individualism; the unbelievable risks those early cowboys took.

I often wondered, in those early years, what had made the bad guys so evil, so mean and heartless, so "crazy." I didn't feel that way about the Indians. I sympathized with them, and I often left the ten-cent Saturday matinee during the massacre of the Indians by the cavalry—always to my buddies' dismay. We were good friends and probably too young to fully recognize and make much of my mixed-blood Ojibwa heritage; they merely grumbled about my not staying for the entire movie, not why I left. I never cared much for the cavalry. They were the crazy bad guys I didn't understand, not the Indians. How had they become crazy bad guys, what had happened to them to make them like that? It must have been something pretty traumatic and intense, that's for sure. I couldn't figure it out, so I focused on the virtues of the white-hatted cowboys who were mavericks of sorts, like the renegade Indians. The good cowboys always seemed to develop special relationships with the Indians—they were "blood brothers."

As my childhood faded into adolescence, my interest in television and movie Westerns dimmed. I came of age during the revolutionary sixties, and there were real shoot-outs and firefights occurring in Vietnam, Alabama, Mississippi, Detroit, Watts, Kent. The white-hatted, good guys were being assassinated: JFK, Malcolm X, King, RFK. College campuses were in a state of unrest, with many of them rescued by the cavalry—the National Guard. No one over thirty was to be trusted; we were the new generation of renegades, mavericks (white hats) fighting for good, justice, the underdog, freedom, new laws, individualism, and risking more than most of us realized at the time. The older generation responded as if we were renegade Indians (to be controlled, pacified, civilized, and in some cases massacred), rather than young mavericks trying to make the world a better place. Some of us were forced into the ranks of the cavalry—the Seventh Calvary, Airborne—and sent to Vietnam to fight the "real" bad guys—the Communists.

When I left the military and returned to graduate school in 1973, I was told that I was a natural counselor, whatever that meant. I took it to mean I was using what I had learned thus far in life to talk with people about their life-problems, to understand their emotions and their thinking, and to help them find solutions to their difficulties. I discovered later that it also meant I did not conform to or emulate any particular theoretical framework or therapeutic approach. I "flew by the seat of my pants," creating as I went along, out there on the edge of the envelope, a nonconformist, a maverick, a "cowboy."

Given the time frame (the mid-1970s), Carl Rogers's client-centered, nondirective approach was still prevalent, along with psychodynamic approaches, humanism, and behaviorism. I was overly directive, intrusive, and asked clients "why" and "how come" questions, when that was taboo. But my professors and clinical supervisors said it seemed to work for me and my clients. I was a natural counselor, whatever that meant. I knew I still didn't know the meaning of "craziness," how and why some clients were crazy, or how to treat craziness or restructure a personality. So, as earlier in my life, I decided to focus on clients who were within the normal range of development and the virtues and goodness of the human potential movement and experiential learning. I learned to recognize psychopathology and to make appropriate referrals. Psychopathology—craziness—was not the territory of cowboy therapists.

I found room for my anomalous style within the psychotherapeutic theories of existentialism, gestalt, and experiential psychotherapy. I also discovered that the intense trauma, abuse, tragedy, and pain my clients experienced were normal problems. I had treated post-traumatic stress disorder (PTSD), as a counselor in the "cavalry" from 1970 to 1973, before it became a diagnostic category in the Diagnostic Statistical Manual. Back then, it was a normal consequence of combat and war. I still didn't know the meaning of "craziness."

Over the past twenty-six years, I have learned that some people do become broken through the normal course of living. I also think I use terms like "crazy" and "broken" because they seem as helpful to my understanding of psychopathology as such terms as schizophrenia, bipolar personality, borderline, ad infinitum. I have also learned that most people are amazingly strong and resistant to "breakage," and that "people are strong, relationships are fragile."

All of this is by way of getting to the role of the psychotherapist in intensive therapy. The therapist needs to be more conventional and traditional when treating clients with diagnosed pathologies, but therapy with nonpathological clients can also be very intense. There is also one important caveat to the following discussion. I am discussing intensive therapy with clients who have *not* been diagnosed as psychopathological. The therapist roles and interventions I suggest are intended for clients who have intense issues in their lives—rape, incest, divorce and child custody, AIDS, death and dying—but who are not psychopathological. I have found that therapy with such clients and issues is often intense, requiring a number of sessions; however, the severity of such problems is most often within the normal range of human development and does not involve psychopathology. To suggest the following interventions and roles with pathological clients could be very harmful, even destructive. To use the old adage: "Never take away their defenses, because there's nothing behind the defenses except an expansive black hole." In addition, to use such roles and interventions with pathological clients would be descriptive of some critics' existing perceptions of therapists as "the-rapists." (Some critics of therapy and therapists view therapy and therapists as harmful to everyone—regardless of the therapists' approach—and have used the term "the-rapist" as a clever play on words to support their criticism.)

Given this caveat, the earlier call for more fighting, risk-taking therapists during the 1960s is still, I think, applicable to the revolutionary therapist of the 1990s and twenty-first century. By this I mean therapists should be social reformers, reaching out to client populations in distress; fighting and advocating for client rights; taking up causes and waving banners as advocates for those in need; and not bound to their offices. Not to contradict my earlier disclaimer (that radical, maverick therapists might be harmfull to diagnosed pathological patients), these therapist roles are equally applicable to fighting for the rights and needs of deinstitutionalized mental patients, who comprise large numbers of homeless in our society.

Many therapists in private practice have untold skills and talents they could use as consultants and educational interventionists in schools, businesses, and communities. The range of opportunities for psychotherapists is limited only by their resourcefulness in translating their skills into services useful to particular organizations or individuals, whether these services are preventive, educational, developmental, or remedial. Resourcefulness means moving out of the office to provide nontraditional services. Otherwise, opportunities for all psychotherapists and mental health professionals will be notably proscribed—by managed health care—if the only services offered are individual or group therapy delivered in the practitioner's private office.

For example, during the 1990s, I spent one day a week in a large urban high school in Hartford, Connecticut, facilitating a therapy group with ninth-grade minority males who were at risk of never completing their high school education. Granted, I didn't always know how to respond to the young group member who stared at the floor to hide his tears as he told me and the other group members that he was afraid. He was afraid because he had lost four of his neighborhood friends to shooting deaths in the past three months. This young man never returned to the group after his disclosure. During the group, in a moment of fear and vulnerability, he disclosed more than his "code of the street" allowed. He admitted a weakness. I still saw the young man every week, individually, and he felt no animosity toward me or the other group members. He was doing well academically and had a chance to make it through school. I remember his saying, "It's okay talking; I'm gonna make it; I just can't go back to that group." He did make it; he graduated at least, even though he never came back to the group.

My group co-facilitator and I didn't know what to do the day that, one by one, the young men got up from the circle and left. Toward the end, only three of them remained in the circle of chairs. As we sat, one of the remaining three turned to my co-facilitator, Matt, and said, "I brought a gun to school yesterday. But, I'm doing better; I didn't bring it today."

Some days, we didn't talk about much of anything, except the latest horror movies, as we sat in our circle and ate doughnuts purchased at the small bakery near our rural university campus, thirty miles away. They didn't like the jelly-filled ones. We usually talked about something important, even if it was only metaphorically. Some days, I lost my composure and objectivity, got angry, and yelled at a group member for his self-defeating behaviors and cocksure fifteen-year-old "attitude." Most days, I returned from the school downhearted.

It often seems so overwhelming and impossible, but not hopeless. These young men aren't crazy. They do in many ways live in the "Wild Wild West," and they do need to learn to trust and depend on others; they do need mentors and models to care for them and to emulate; they do need people to listen and respond to their fears, their pain, and their rage; they do need to hope that their lives can be better.

On balance, these young, urban high school men seemed to respond well to this gray, long-haired, mixed-blood guy from the rural university campus thirty miles away. Maybe they saw I was still a maverick of sorts, that I came from a place very similar to their own, and that I was with them one day a week because I wanted to be there. Maybe it was because I felt good knowing there were still places for cowboy therapists to be helpful, and these young men appreciated that I wanted to ride into their territory and be with them. I can't help but believe many more cowboy therapists are needed and would be welcomed.

Working in contexts such as these, and with young men such as these, I have learned some additional things about being a risk-taking, revolutionary (cowboy) therapist.

As Coles (1993) states so well, in describing his volunteer teaching experience with eleventh-graders in an urban high school in Boston: "I'd learned in psychiatric and psychoanalytic training the importance of putting one's cards on the table, of telling a story or two, of explaining oneself as a means of helping others pay attention (and earning their trust). . . . I was struggling for a moral authority that would be theirs as well—that would break the hold of fear and anger on their part and, on mine, the fear of failure and anger at my vulnerability" (p. A52).

I have learned there are times when these young people need to be supported or hugged (sometimes literally); there are other times when they need to be confronted and challenged or kicked and pushed (metaphorically); there are still other times when they need to be left alone or ignored (what I call benign neglect).

The difficulty, of course, is knowing who needs which intervention, when, how much, and for how long. Obviously, I made mistakes with these young people. Flying by the seat of one's pants sometimes leads to mistakes. But with experience, I found that I was on target more than I was missing with these young men.

I continued to drive my 1990 Ford Mustang each week to and from the school in Hartford. I named the Ford Mustang "Horse," as in "A Horse with No Name" from the 1971 America album, *America* (Samwell, Dexter, Bunnell, Beckley, and Peek 1971).

I've been through the desert on a horse with no name
It felt good to be out of the rain . . .
In the desert you can remember your name because
there ain't no one for to give you no pain . . .
It made me feel sad to think it was dead . . .
I let the horse go free, because the desert had turned
to sea . . .
I was looking at all the life . . .
There were plants and birds and rocks and things . . .
There was sand and hills and rain . . .
Under the cities lies a heart made of ground . . .
But the humans will give no love.

My son gave me the audiotape of the America album, and I listened to its lyrics as I drove back and forth to the urban high school in Hartford. My son was in college studying to be an educator, majoring in sociology and psychology. When I drove, I often thought there were still a few boys who dreamed of being cowboys when they grew up—riding through deserts and cities with hearts made of ground, turning them to sea.

Chapter 12

Wizards, Dragons, and 'prentices

The military police found Marc's body slumped on a bench in the Gardenplatz, near the officers' housing complex where he lived in Heidelberg, Federal Republic of Germany. A note was pinned to the left breast pocket of his BDUs (battle dress uniform), just below his nametag. The police blotter said he had a single bullet hole to the head, a shot fired from a Czechoslovak pistol at close range—cause of death: suicide.

Marc was one of my students in an overseas program in counseling psychology, and a major in the United States Army. The note on his pocket said that he could no longer go on, he was not a good example for his two preschool-aged sons to model, and he was an embarrassment to the U.S. Army, his family, and his wife, who was a lieutenant colonel in the Army. Twice, Marc had been passed over for lieutenant colonel and was forced to leave the military or to take a reduction in rank. He had been raised in a career Army family and had attended a private military academy before becoming a soldier himself. The Army was his life and his identity, although he was a compassionate and caring man and atypical of the gung ho stereotype of a career military officer. Regardless, being passed over for promotion was beyond his ability to cope.

Before Marc's death, the two of us had played racquetball together at least three, and often four, times a week at the nearby military installation. I was aware of Marc's situation and his difficult decision, although I did not cross our professional teacher-student boundaries, despite my ability to do so and the significant amount of out-of-class time we spent together. I listened mostly while driving to and from the racquetball courts.

Meanwhile the old, white-bearded, bushy eyebrowed wizard sits silent upon his wooden throne, draped in a floor-length robe of spun gold and jewels, with a slight forward sag to the tip of his high pointy hat. He extends the open palm of one empty hand and gently balances a ball of glass in the other, staring blankly into the distance. Across the room sits another more modest and tacit wizard, clothed in a burlap wrap cinched with common rope. Although he too is bearded in white with tangles of brow, he rubs the baldness of his crown with one hand as he studies the reflections of a much smaller crystal globe in the other. No magic wands, no fairy dust, no prophetic tales, no profound words, no enchanted glass, no mysterious chants . . . no wizardry here, only the images of a European artisan crafted in porcelain figurines.

Some thirteen years later, I still wish I had done more than sit in silence and listen to Marc. And I wish I had had the wisdom to cross those professional boundaries between us. Despite this lesson, and after twenty-six years as an educator and supervisor of therapists, I continue to struggle with the personal-professional boundaries. My colleagues continually warn me of the ethics of dual relationships and the differences among teaching, supervising, mentoring, and counseling students as they learn to be therapists. They say I am in a position of power in my role as professor and evaluator of my students' academic and clinical performance, and that I am not to cross the lines of teaching and therapy. Here be dragons! But, I think to myself, they know nothing of Marc, or the art and wizardry of therapy—and teaching.

I don't believe we can legitimately talk about learning the trade of psychotherapy without also focusing on how therapy is currently taught, and how that teaching and learning has changed over the years. Sometimes I think I am becoming, or have already become, out of step, someone who glorifies the past and remembers only the good parts.

I learned to be a therapist with the Mueller and Kell (1972) training and supervision model. Based on this model, when I was a wannabe therapist, I needed to become aware of and resolve the parallel processes among my personal relationships and those with my clients and supervisors. It was more than transference and countertransference, or parataxic distortions, to use Sullivan's description; it was the realization that I could not possibly form therapeutic and helpful relationships with my clients unless and until I acknowledged and resolved personal issues and conflicts in my own relationships—be they familial, romantic, friendly, or whatever. And the way to cope with and resolve these conflicts was through supervision and my own personal therapy.

The critical aspect of Mueller and Kell's model was that the supervisor, who was also typically the student's academic professor, served all three roles: teacher, supervisor, and therapist. Of course, there was always the option for the student of therapy to seek his or her own therapist, someone other than the academic professor and supervisor. But, make no mistake, undergoing therapy was a requirement, not an option, of learning the trade.

Today, most academic professors of psychotherapy can no longer require that therapists-in-training receive personal therapy—we can only suggest it. And, for the most part, academic professors hardly supervise their students. Instead, students are farmed out to internship placements, and the field supervisors provide clinical supervision. In fact, Haley (1996) contends—and I agree—that today's academic training of therapists has little correlation with students becoming skilled therapists and clinicians. Clinical training and education occur separate from academic programs, via pre- or postdoctoral internship placements. Haley also notes something of which I was unaware, but suspected: in most medical school curricula for psychiatric residents, clinical training in one-to-one or group therapy is an elective, not a requirement. Such clinical training and education have been replaced by the study of psychopharmacology and neuropsychology—the scientific, medical definition of clinician. And, to no one's surprise, there is no requirement that psychiatrists undergo personal therapy themselves.

Nevertheless, the world has moved on. Marc is gone, and I was not able to save him. I didn't even try to work magic; like the wizards carved in porcelain, I sat in silence. Yet, I still aspire to be a wizard: a master and mentor of my art and trade as I attempt to teach others to be the same. But, there be dragons! Gone, for the most part, are the wizards and the magic they work; gone are the knights and squires, and the valiant battles they fought to overcome the fears embodied in their dragons of old; gone, too, are the mavericks, the renegades, the cowboys, the gunslingers, the barnstormers, the freedom riders, the heros and heroines—and their dreams and artisanship, I fear.

The world has moved on and, in my view, my colleagues have become more concerned about political correctness, litigation, consumer satisfaction, credentialing, accreditation standards and approval, health care providers, and related matters of the profession. My dilemma has been whether to move on with the world—and with them—or to hold on to the magic of being a psychotherapist and teaching others the art of the trade. And, there be dragons!

Despite my relentless doubts about being an anachronistic prima donna, and a dinosaur on the brink of extinction, I have decided to fight the dragons, old and new, to aspire to be a wizard of my trade, and to try to work the magic of goodness, truth, equality, compassion, harmony, and balance—with my clients and my students. Perhaps as a child—and as an adult—I read too much Tolkien and believed too much in Camelot, Avalon, King Arthur and his champion knight Lancelot, wizards, hobbits, dragons, sorcerers, heroic cowboys and Indians saving the day, and evil as the world moved on without me. But, for the most part, I think not: damned be the dragons! Besides, to be a valued knight and hero, a dragonslayer needs formidable dragons as opponents to conquer.

Maybe this is how I continue to believe that I have something of value to teach students of psychotherapy, by seeing myself as a champion of the traditional ways. I truly believe that there is value in the old ways of learning to be a psychotherapist, and that if some of us do not continue to teach and live what we learned from the old masters, the art and craft of psychotherapy will be lost to technology, science, pharmaceutical companies, geneticists—the new age dragons.

Don't misunderstand: I also realize there is much to be gained from the modern advancements in the practice of psychotherapy. It is not using these new tools and technologies that I object to; it is the lack of balance between the old and the new. Just as the time had come for the new era of the technological and information age to replace the Industrial Age, it may well be the time for a new era of psychotherapy. But, as in earlier times, something is lost as well: the blacksmith transforming lead into steel, the woodworker making a chair from the stump of a tree or a canoe from the bark of a birch tree, the artisan carving a figurine from soapstone or a peace pipe from the red stone of Minnesota. With the loss of the masters who taught the apprentices, the art and craft of their hearts, souls, spirits, and trade was lost as well. And, there be dragons!

I recall my exit interview with my major advisor and mentor when I finished my doctorate and formal training as a therapist. During my academic and clinical training, it was not uncommon for him to cross professional boundaries between teacher-student and therapist-client. I am still grateful that he did. In this spirit, my advisor and mentor told me during my exit interview that he thought I would be a masterful therapist, but that he also had some significant concerns about my professional and personal development. He was concerned about my professional maturity, as he called it. That is, he was concerned that I was still too much of a dreamer and not enough of a realist. He was concerned that I would be significantly hurt, professionally and personally, by refusing to compromise my ideals. The world wasn't the way I believed it was or should be. I had harsh realities ahead of me, he said, ones that I would have to face and learn from. He prophesied that I would be fired from several positions, and resign from others, based on my naive ideals and beliefs. As I left his office, he gave me a small pewter dragon and warmly told me to "watch out for the dragons," and that I should call him any time I needed to talk. His was a powerful crystal indeed. There have been many dragons, and his prophesy has certainly come true. I have been fired three times and resigned twice over the last twenty-six years. And I did talk with him—a lot—before his death from cancer. I named the pewter dragon he gave me "Marty," in remembrance of him.

I began what would become a tradition over the years with my own students, based on my exit interview with my mentor. At their graduation, I gave each of them a pewter dragon and the following bit of text, rolled into a scroll:

> The Dragon
>
> One last goodbye from your Alma Mater, the Counseling Psychology Program, and me. I think this symbol of the dragon is the most appropriate thing I can give to you at graduation. In a way, it's the continuation of a tradition started back-in-the-day by a beloved mentor and colleague of my own, who gave to me a similar dragon—to keep me idealistic, committed to my cause, and to wave the banner of my own convictions and Alma Mater. It may symbolize myself to some of you. To others it may embody your own fears, past and present.
>
> We had many dragon fights among ourselves during our years together, and we breathed a little fire at each other occasionally. But, I think it made you, and

> me, a little stronger and better for it. And, there will inevitably be meaner dragons than I, out there, in the Real World. Remember to watch for their tails, they find you when you're least suspecting. But, you're as ready as we can get you—to fight the real dragons waiting to face you.
>
> Keeping with tradition, the first thing you need to do is to give your dragon a name; second, keep her or him in a safe place; and third, and most important, any time you're feeling discouraged, losing your commitment and convictions, and the banner is faltering, gently rub your dragon and something magical will happen: to restore your idealism, your cause and commitment, and your remembrance of our time and the banner we flew together. Remember, a Good Dragon is the only one who knows how to fight for and protect you from the Evil Dragons you will face.
>
> Keep the Light My Friends,
> Michael

I mention all of this because it is part of my dilemma about holding on to the traditional ways of teaching and learning therapy and my continuing struggle with the personal-professional boundaries of teaching, mentoring, and therapy. I stopped giving graduating therapists pewter dragons and the accompanying scroll in 1994. The world had moved on, and so had many of the wannabe therapists I was teaching and supervising. These students were no longer seeking a mentor, nor were they interested in learning the art of psychotherapy. Instead, they were seeking credentials, entreé to the world of third-party payments and managed health care, the biggest payoff for the least amount of effort, the easy way to becoming a therapist: go to class, take the test, write the paper, do the internship, pass go, and enter private practice or institutional counseling. And, regardless of my recommendations and suggestions, none of them wanted or needed therapy themselves. The magic was gone; they wanted only the right techniques and cookbook texts on the how-to of therapy, neuropsychology, and technology.

Despite my efforts to convince them of the magic involved in learning to be masterful therapists, they would hear nothing of it. In retrospect, and had I it to do over again, I would not have persisted and continued my efforts to convince them and demonstrate the artistic value of therapy. Although I knew the world had moved on, and was aware of the professional risks of continuing my efforts, I continued nevertheless. The long and short of it is that I was profoundly hurt as a result, by the students for whom I cared and in whom I invested so much of myself, as well as by those colleagues who had warned me about blurring the professional lines between teaching, mentoring, and therapy. In response, I withdrew physically and emotionally—to recover, feel, heal, and rethink my place in the world of teaching and learning therapy.

I rediscovered *Voices*, a journal that still believes in the art of psychotherapy, and I began to write for it. I worked out many of my feelings, and rethought my place in the profession, through writing. The writing of Getman (1992), a law professor at the University of Texas, also retaught me, as Mueller and Kell first taught me some twenty-eight years ago, that it is through personal involvement and emotional engagement with those students who are seeking a mentor and an apprenticeship that I have the most to contribute. I believe I have come to a good place in my healing process, and an occasional 'prentice does enter my life.

'Prentices become wizards by first slaying their own dragons, suffering the defeats as well as enjoying the victories in their own process of learning the art. I have learned there are as few proteges in psychotherapy as there are in other disciplines and domains. For most of us, becoming a master of our trade is a process of hard work and learning. Haley (1996) has also said that he has never met a master therapist under the age of fifty. Perhaps I agree with Haley's perspective because it gives me solace and hope that I may still become a master and wizard of therapy. I am now fifty-five.

Further, I have come to realize that there were many among us learners, then, just as there are today, who had no interest in serving as apprentices or being mentored in the trade. They too were collecting the appropriate credentials, writing the papers, taking the tests, doing the internships, passing go, and entering the profession in the easiest way possible. Not all those who learn the trade of psychotherapy want to or become masters of the craft. I remember the old nature-nurture debates during my time as a 'prentice, and those professors and mentors who would say, "You can't make a silk purse out of a sow's ear."

All in all, though, I think my mentor would be pleased with how I have matured professionally since our exit interview so many years ago. I have learned important lessons from the harsh realities I have faced: the hazards of sitting in silence, the dangers of charging dragons naively and idealistically, and the importance of harmony and balance between the two. And, with the exception of those like Marc, I believe the errors I have made—for the most part—have been in the right direction, leading toward realistic idealism and preserving the art and practice of the trade as it was taught to me.

I received a letter once from a former student, a young man who was one of the last of whom I had given a pewter dragon at graduation. He included a clipping from the *Westwood Press* (June 26, 1997), a suburban Boston publication, that included the following:

Students and parents crowded the high school music room at Thursday's School Committee meeting to plead for the return of a beloved counselor. . . . The decision to not make room in the budget for [his] position was made by the school Principal. "I think I could go to him with any problem I have," said a junior at the high school and one of 300 students who signed a petition for [his] return. One parent read a statement with tears in her eyes about how [he] helped her daughter when she was dealing with the death of a good friend. Another student said [he] had come to her home to talk to her older sister about an eating disorder.

In his accompanying letter, the young man indicated that his position had been reinstated and that he was still a counselor at his school. He also wrote, "Well, I guess it is time to move on to the next project of the day. I hope you enjoyed hearing from me. Although I have not been good about staying in touch, I do think about you often. I've had a few dragons to fight. Love, James."

We don't always get what we want, but we usually get what we need. The young man's letter serves to reaffirm my need to believe that there is still a place for the old ways in learning psychotherapy, that there are still students who are seeking an apprenticeship with a beloved mentor, and those who wish to become masters of their trade. And it may well be good for those who are learning to be therapists to know that there remain a few aging, wannabe wizards, with pewter dragons perched upon a window sill, waiting eagerly for young 'prentices to enter their lives in search of a mentor to teach them the magic and art of psychotherapy, and with whom to carry their banners and slay some dragons.

Chapter 13

Barn's Burnt Down . . . Now I Can See the Moon

> Every time I look at the lake now, I smile and my eyes well up with tears. I can feel your spirit touch me. Memories, the things that you hold close to your heart. You are always on the deck looking out at the water. Look at the moon tonight and think of us and I will be looking at it and thinking of you. The moon is bright tonight and reflecting off the water. Thanks for being my Pops, my father, and my friend.

My son Ross wrote these words to me in the fall of 1998, following my visit with him in northern Michigan—he is one who keeps the faith in my heart and my and spirit and soul alive.

Even though I was a nonswimmer, from the age of eight to twelve, I nonetheless got in line each summer with the intent of climbing the wooden slats nailed to the trunk of the aged oak tree and diving into the Grand River from the board wedged high in the crotch of the tree's large branches. Each year, as I stood in front of the tree for my turn to climb, I stepped away, to the jeers of the other boys and an occasional tomboy, and let the next in line climb to the platform and dive into the river. Every summer I swore to myself that I would learn to swim, and next year would be the year I would dive. I didn't learn to swim until I went to college, and I never dived from the plank of the old oak tree. I always stepped away.

In other aspects of my life, however, I embraced the challenges presented to me. I could run fast and had moderate athletic ability, so every summer, instead of diving and swimming in the river, I spent my time playing baseball, shooting baskets, jumping hurdles, and throwing the football around. Although my heart was bigger than my abilities, I nevertheless excelled in athletics, obtaining a varsity letter in track for four years and lettering for three years in basketball and football, as well as being captain or co-captain of each of the three teams. I also excelled academically, despite the fact that I did not do well on standardized tests and was placed in the noncollege-bound track in junior high. By my freshman year in high school, I had a B+ to A- average and was promoted to the college-bound classes—whatever that meant; I had no financial means of attending college.

Things worked out, and my willingness to embrace the challenges presented to me was rewarded by athletic and academic scholarships to attend college. I never told anyone that it was my heart and not my abilities that motivated me to confront the challenges—except for the oak tree that overhung the Grand River. My first semester at college, I learned that everyone was required to take a specified number of physical education classes, whether or not he or she was a collegiate athlete. And one of the required P.E. classes was swimming. I enrolled in that course my first semester, and my first class meeting was at the pool. Physical education classes were not co-educational back then, so we were all boys. For hygiene purposes they said, everyone took a shower before entering the pool area and no one wore swimming trunks. To assess each class member's swimming proficiency, the instructor had the entire class line up at the deep end of the pool. When it was your turn at the edge of the pool you were supposed to say, "Swimmer," and jump into the pool and swim, or say, "Nonswimmer," and step away from the edge of the pool. When it came my turn, standing naked with everyone else, I yelled, "Nonswimmer," and jumped into the pool. I immediately sank to the bottom of the fifteen-foot-deep pool as the instructor and his aids dived in after me, clothes and all, pulling me from the pool gagging and spitting water from my mouth and nose. As the instructor yelled at me for not complying with his instructions, I kept saying, "I'm never stepping away again." Although to this day I am not a strong swimmer, I did learn to swim that semester, and I forgot about stepping away—for a time.

I learned much later in life that my Native American elders advise four ways of approaching life's challenges and the negative energy often associated with them: you can let it in and have it harm you, you can deflect or redirect it, you can confront it, or you can step away. Because I was always sensitive as a kid, and still am as an adult—in that it mattered what people said to me, about me, or about what was important to me—I too often let in the negative energy of challenges and it harmed me. Although I grew up in the Midwest, where it was common to hear people say, "It don't mean nothin', it don't matter, it don't bother me none," I was never able to deflect or redirect the negative energy of life's challenges in this way. And, even though as a young boy stepping away from the oak tree, I still let in the negative energy to harm me—the raillery of others diminished my self-confidence as a result. To avoid the harm of letting in the negative energy when I stepped away, and because I couldn't or didn't know how to deflect or redirect the negativity, I learned to confront only the other challenges presented to me.

As the years have gone by, however, the challenges of life and my continual confrontation of them have worn through the protective covering of my faith to expose its inner most depths. Sometimes I have felt that I have finally burned out, that I have grown tired of doing what I am doing, that the losses outnumber the victories, that there are more punishments than rewards for standing up to the challenges, that it is time to pass the baton to the next generation, that I really have not and cannot make the differences in peoples' lives that I once thought I could. In these times of negative reflective thinking, I inevitably would focus on those patients and students with whom I did not make a difference, those who did not succeed in attaining their goals, who did not graduate, who did not overcome their life problems, who did not change, who did not get better and, in some cases, those who did not live.

In going to this doubting place of my innermost beliefs, I have come to know that without these challenges I would not have realized the positive strength of my faith in myself and how I am with others. I have come to know that I did not truly step away from that old oak tree on the banks of the Grand River. I let in and carried old hurts with me for years, I deflected challenges by redirecting my efforts to areas where I was fairly certain I could succeed, and I stood up to and confronted the negative energy of earlier life challenges by proving myself to others or proving others wrong. I have also come to know that the challenges to my faith are not about winning and losing, burning out, getting tired, passing batons, external punishments and rewards, or counting the number of times I make a difference in someone's life. Challenges to faith are about staying alive emotionally, intellectually, and physically and finding the balance among these life-giving and life-taking forces.

I have come to know that my faith in how I am with others, and in myself, has to do with connecting. It has to do with connecting to others, connecting to nature, connecting to my surroundings, connecting to my feelings and thoughts, connecting to my innermost spirit and soul—what I value, what I believe, whom I love and who is important to me, what it is in life that matters to me—how I am with people, not what I have accomplished or what I do. The elders say, "A person is known by what he does, a person is respected by how he is with others." These may be simple and obvious understandings and knowings for many; but, for me, learning how and when to connect—and disconnect—has not come easily.

My experience with an erstwhile client points out the healing results of connection as a goal of therapy. Kim was a young woman from Taiwan whose presenting problem was one of language and adjustment to Western culture. The English language was a barrier for her, mostly in that others could not understand her English; she understood others' English just fine. For whatever reasons, I had no problem understanding Kim's English, and we communicated very easily from the first session.

For several sessions we focused on the presenting problem and its effect on her feelings of self-worth, confidence, and competence. A normally gregarious and outspoken young woman in her native country, she had become quiet, unsure of herself, self-doubting, and somewhat of a recluse since moving to the United States three years before. However, our focus on language as the problem, albeit the presenting one, became the obstacle to my seeing and making the more important and healing connection to Kim.

I finally told her I did not feel the two of us were connecting the way I would like and that perhaps we should explore some new territory. With tears in her eyes, she extended her right hand in front of her, palm facing me, as if indicating for me to stop, dropped her head to her chest, and began to cry. "What, what?" I asked. She proceeded to tell me that in her culture if a woman has a midline on her right palm that extends across the entire width of the hand, then she will be unhappy in marriage and unsuccessful as a mother. The midline of Kim's right hand crossed the entire palm. Kim was also married, to a Taiwanese man, but she and her husband were currently in the midst of significant conflict over whether to have a first child. Kim said she could not be a mother because of the line on her palm. Her own mother had likewise reinforced this belief, over and over again, from a very early age. Kim told me she was crying because I had said we were not connecting. Except for her father, she felt more connected to me than anyone else in her life. If not, she said, why would she have shown me the palm of her hand? Not even her husband or best friends knew about her palm.

I apologized to Kim and told her that she was right to cry about my hurtful comment. A relationship between people depends on, involves, and follows from each other. In other words, it is reciprocal, two-way, flowing from each partner to the other in the relationship/connection. I had seen our relationship only from my perspective. As I reflected silently on our previous sessions, images came to mind of Kim sitting always with her right hand hidden: under the flank of a leg, squeezed beneath an arm, or covered by the palm of her left hand as both hands lay in her lap.

During the next several months, Kim and I worked on disconnecting, separating, and detaching her negative value of herself from the myth of her hand, and her related connections to this problem. As is typical for me, I often walk and sit with my clients out-of-doors. I use these surroundings to help clients make other, healthier connections—to nature and, most times, to their feelings and thoughts. Kim was no exception. We often sat on the stoop of a building or on a bench during our therapy sessions outside. I told her I knew almost nothing of her culture, that connections are based on what we share in common, and that I could not connect with the difference of her hand. I remember during one particular session that I looked at a tree and asked if she knew what kind of tree it was. She did. I also remember saying something like, "We can breach our individual differences through our connections. You know, each of that tree's individual leaves is different from the other, no two are exactly alike. But, they are all similar in that they're connected to the same tree. There also comes a time when the tree casts off its leaves and begins anew. It's part of the balance and harmony of things, that no amount of our interference can change. The tree must shed its old leaves if it is to grow and stay alive."

Kim reached across her body with her right hand to grasp mine, and said, "That sounds like something my father would say." I smiled. The healing connection had begun.

To me, such connections are the way to right relationships and are at the very heart of my faith in psychotherapy. By this I mean the importance and healing effect of connection as the way to right relationships with others—and with oneself. Nevertheless, there have been times when life's challenges have created self-doubt and made me question my faith in psychotherapy. Until 1995, I continued the way to right relationships by connecting to others and confronting the challenges. But things changed again, and a new challenge presented itself. It was a personal and professional challenge that would require me to revisit the advice of my elders and to learn once more, for myself, the real meaning of stepping away, and the way for me to stay connected to my faith in psychotherapy.

I sometimes become nostalgic and long for times past. But, there is also reality in the nostalgia; I know things do change over time. As a professor and educator of therapists (reaffirmed by Getman 1992), I have seen university controversies ebb and flow, and the specific issues at any given moment change. In the 1960s, there was conflict over free speech, students marched and staged protests over military adventurism, civil rights, academe's involvement in war-related research, and the imperatives of shared governance and participatory democracy. In the 1970s, debates ensued over feminism, ethnic studies programs, women's studies, affirmative action mandates, and university investments in countries marked by repressive regimes. The past two decades have included disputes over hate speech codes on campus, gay and lesbian rights, multiculturalism, the curricular canon, sexual harassment, political correctness, professional ethics, faculty tenure, new technologies, accreditation, and the soaring costs of education.

Things have likewise changed for psychotherapy. The human potential movement of the 1960s and the experiential search for self-knowledge and connection, which nicely matched the goals and purposes of psychotherapy, have given way to the positivistic scientists' focus on neuropsychology, genetics, and medical and pharmaceutical prescriptions and proscriptions for treatment. The escalating costs of medical care have resulted in managed health care and controversy over insurance panels, the number of allowed therapy sessions, allowable fees for services delivered, credentialing and accreditation, appropriate training and educational levels for therapists, and licensure of therapists from competing disciplines: marriage and family therapy, social work, mental health counseling, school psychology, clinical psychology, counseling psychology, and so on.

At my university, these changes in education and mental health care merged to form a critical break point in 1995—a turbulent crash of swirling, twisting, eddying currents at the fork in the river. The rising costs of education, the competition among similar education programs on campus, and strategic planning committees that established university mission statements, resource allocations, and areas of excellence brought my training program under siege. Once again, I took up the challenge and defended my belief and faith in psychotherapy and my program's training of therapists. The siege was lessened, for a while, until 1998.

During this three-year period, everything became politicized, and even the smallest event or incident became grossly petty and exaggerated. An offhand remark by the university's chief executive officer, a memo distributed by the dean or department head, an informal exchange between two colleagues as they passed in the hallway, and the most casual comment became grist for the rumor mill and was held up to scrutiny and examined for whatever covert significance it contained. Hidden agendas were suspected everywhere, and jockeying for position, status, and influence was constant. Obviously, in such highly charged and politicized situations, personalities were also involved and I could not avoid the politics entirely. Nonetheless, I stood my ground and confronted the challenge to my profession, and held fast to my faith in the healing effect of connection to others.

Despite prolonging for three years the closing of my training program, I remember my own breaking point—when I was swallowed up in the whirlpool of torrents at the fork in the river—in the winter of 1995. I was sitting on the edge of my bed, examining the latest flurry of interoffice memos, trying to compose my response in defense of the program and in defense of myself. I looked up from the papers strewn on the bed as Janice entered the bedroom. I had tears in my eyes and my body was shaking visibly with anxiety and fear. "I need your help, I need your help with this, I can't do this anymore."

She walked over to the bed, sat down next to me, and gently held me as I let out the tears in the soft hollow between her shoulder and neck. "You never ask me for help Michael, even when you need to ask me. How can I help?" She drove me to the university late that night to make copies of some meaningless—in retrospect—memo in response to those I had been examining on the bed. On the way, I told her of my decision to resign as coordinator of the training program. She told me that she thought the decision was the best thing for me, but that she was sad that so much good would be lost. I resigned at the end of the fall semester in 1995, and the program limped along until the spring of 1998, when the official announcement was made that it was to be phased out.

It took me almost those entire three years to finally step away from that tree. During that time, I went to the doubting place of my innermost faith and negative reflective thinking. I remember looking at a picture taken of me during this period, and being appalled by the depressed and despondent face staring back at me. That visual image jarred and loosened me from my self-imposed doubt and negativity. I gradually began to see again my confident connection to others, to nature, to my surroundings, to my feelings and thoughts, to my innermost spirit and faith. I also came to know that part of connecting is disconnecting—what the elders call stepping away.

This positive knowing was mostly synchronous and serendipitous. As fate might have it, we have two old oak trees in our back yard. One is considered to be the oldest and largest in the city. I had observed for two summers, however, that the other younger and smaller oak tree's leaves were infested with a parasite. The leeches destroyed the leaves, curling them at the edges until they finally died and eventually dropped from their branches. I pruned the lower branches, thinking that might help, and looked from the upstairs bathroom window each morning for any improvement in the tree's condition. What I observed was that each time the parasites destroyed the leaves, new ones sprouted from the tree's branches. I observed this cyclical process at least three times over the course of that summer. One afternoon, as I stood looking from my deck at the tree, I thought to myself, "This tree has been here for more than one hundred years, it has survived a hurricane in the 1930s, it has survived cold winters, summer droughts, floods, and who knows how many prior infestations of parasites. It is strong, vibrant, and alive. . . . It will most certainly survive and thrive without my consternation or interference. I need to step away and let it be."

I also remembered my elders speaking of the importance of connection and harmony with all things, and my similar insights about trees and the comments I had made to Kim during one of our outdoor therapy sessions. As an ironical aside—that now brings a smile to my face—the university's new logo is the oak leaf.

At the end of that summer, in 1998, I also took a trip to northern Michigan to visit with my son, Ross; his young woman, Jodi; and their husky dog, Nyska. They lived in a beautiful part of the state, although remote to say the least, and they had recently purchased a small starter house, with a wonderful view of Otsego Lake. Although Ross and I did some very enjoyable father-son projects together, like building a deck on their house, I settled into a routine each morning and evening of sitting on the back steps looking out at the lake, and watching the sun set and the moon rise in the evening. Ross and Jodi would always join me at the beginning and ending of each day, as would Nyska—she would lick my face, bite my hair, drink from my coffee cup, and filch my pack of cigarettes so that I would chase her. Mostly though, I was just with them, and they with me, connected to each other in a spiritual way that none of us ever talked about. The focus was not on what we did, what we accomplished, or what we were going to do—we were merely with each other. I kissed the dog on the nose and relished her energy and spirit, we all sat together on the steps, we looked out at the lake, we talked when someone had something to say, we watched the sun set and the moon rise.

Before I returned to Connecticut, we also connected their computer to the Internet so that we could send electronic mail messages to one another. After my return, I received the following in a series of messages from my son:

> "Every time I look at the lake now, I smile and my eyes well up with tears. Memories, the things you hold close to your heart. . . . You are always on our deck looking out at the water. . . . The fog was thick over the lake this morning, as I left for practice. In fact, you couldn't even see the water . . . the air was so crisp. Yet, I found myself once again taking a moment to look out upon the water, struggling as I may to see it. Strange as it may seem, by doing so, I can feel your spirit touch me. It means so much to me that [we] were able to spend that time with you. Your energy remains ever present in our home and in our hearts. Thanks for being my Pops, my father, and my friend. . . . Look at the moon tonight and think of us, and I will be looking at it and thinking of you. The moon is bright tonight and reflecting off the water. . . . You know, I wasn't sure why I told you to look at the moon, and then a couple of days ago it came to me . . . "Cat's in the Cradle/Little Boy Blue/ Man in the Moon." Strange how the mind works, isn't it? Know that we are thinking of you and loving you.

I have no better words than his to describe the strength and effect of connection, be it the healing outcome and goal of therapy or in our ordinary, everyday lives.

Not long ago, I characterized myself as a racehorse, living in an academic barn and constrained by the university's external stipulations, controls, administrative micro-management, faculty politics, and hidden agendas. Then, a doctoral student stopped by the house to work with me on her dissertation proposal. She brought with her a greeting card she had made for me, with the inscription, "Barn's Burnt Down . . . Now You Can See the Moon." She and Ross are right: at the heart of who I am as a therapist and person is my spirit and my faith in how I am with people—connecting with them and letting them in, confronting the challenges of life and, sometimes, disconnecting and stepping away from that which I no longer choose to let in, deflect, or confront—things over which I have no control, things I should let be and not interfere with. This is what keeping my faith in psychotherapy and connecting to others—and life itself—is all about. The barn's burnt down . . . now I can see the moon.

Chapter 14

The Art of Failing as a Therapist

Since our first meeting in Tucson, Michael Tlanusta Garrett and I have become close, dear colleagues and friends—like family, nephew and uncle—despite the geographical distance between us. When he asked recently what I was writing about these days, I told him that I was working on a piece about the success or failure of psychotherapy and client suicide. As is typical of Michael and his Cherokee way, he was silent for a long while and then told a story—about learning the art of failing as a therapist.

> A Cherokee man who had been struggling with his direction and purpose in life finally came to a clear point in his confusion and headed off on his life-journey. He walked for many years in the direction that he had chosen for his life and one day approached a high, narrow footbridge that spanned a deep, deep canyon below. On the opposite side of the bridge stood another man, with a long rope tied and wrapped around his waist. As the two men met at the center of the bridge, the Rope man asked the Cherokee man if he would hold the end

> of his rope, very close to its stub, to which the Cherokee man agreed. With disbelief, the Cherokee man watched as the other man went to the edge of the bridge and jumped off, dangling at the limit of the rope that the Cherokee man grasped tightly in his hands. "Please, please," said the Cherokee man, "climb up the rope to the bridge." "Please, please," said the Rope man, "don't let go of the end of the twine or I will surely die." Try as he may, the Cherokee man could not pull the Rope man to the safety of the bridge, for the bridge was too narrow and his hands were too close to the end of the cord. After many days of listening to and talking with the Rope man, pleading with the man to draw himself to safety, holding his end of the rope, the Cherokee man—his hands shaking, raw, and bleeding—and unable to pull the man to the bridge, let go of his end of the rope, turned, and crossed the bridge on his journey.

I first read Jay Haley's tongue-in-cheek monograph on all the wrong things to do in therapy to insure failure, "The Art of Being a Failure as a Therapist," during my master's degree training. I found the piece humorous at the time because of its sarcasm and obviously antithetical advice concerning how to do therapy. As with most acerbic advice and humor, however, there were elements of truth, knowledge, and seriousness involved that I was too naive to appreciate. Although I have misplaced Haley's monograph in the intervening years, suicides by a former student and three patients have forced me to confront my feelings of failure as a therapist. I don't know if four suicides during the better part of twenty-six years doing therapy is typical for most therapists, but I do know it feels like failure, and I think there is an art to learning something from these experiences. For those interested in numbers, approximately 31,000 suicides occur in the United States each year, an estimated 5,000 of which are under the care of a therapist or had been within thirty days of committing suicide. It is also estimated that the number of therapists affected each year by client suicide can range from 5,000 to 15,000.

At times I have thought that my own experience with client suicide was partially a consequence of the high-risk clients and students with whom I worked, and I have rationalized suicide itself with the familiar clichés: "It's not a matter of 'if,' it's a matter of 'when'"; "There are two kinds of therapists: those who have lost a patient to suicide and those who will." None of this has helped much with the guilt, shame, incompetence, and failure I have felt each time. I read something recently that reaffirmed my belief that people are messy and unpredictable, and that being a therapist is no profession for those who do not learn to deal with ambiguity, unknowns, and intense feelings—the seaminess of life's messes and failures.

My first direct experience with suicide came early in my years as a therapist, right after I completed my doctorate and was director of the counseling center at a small liberal arts college in Ohio. The young woman I was seeing was one of several new clients my first semester at the college. There did not appear to be anything out of the ordinary as we progressed through the routine intake session and the objective, diagnostic testing that was required of all students wishing to use the college's counseling services. She seemed to me to be a fairly typical adolescent, struggling to find independence from her parents, occasionally quibbling with her boyfriend, arguing with a roommate over borrowed clothing, drinking a little too much at Saturday night's fraternity party. She was an undecided major, as a junior, which was also not that unusual in the mid-1970s—or now for that matter. She loved anything artistic: painting, music, theater, dance, writing and poetry, and especially photography. We had not been focusing on anything particularly disturbing or troublesome to her, yet the things we discussed did seem important: normal developmental issues and tasks that were helpful for her to say aloud and discuss with someone.

By my second semester at the college, my caseload had grown to the point that I no longer had openings for occasional drop-ins; an appointment was now required. The young woman was scheduled to see me late in the afternoon, on a Friday, but when I went to the receptionist's desk to greet her for her appointment, my secretary said she had dropped by the office about thirty minutes before her appointment, canceled and rescheduled for the following week, and left a beautiful color photograph for me, one that she had taken and developed in the darkroom herself, of a wooded place near campus where students often went to party on weekends.

Two police officers came to my on-campus residence that Sunday following the young woman's canceled appointment. Neither her boyfriend nor her roommates had seen her since Friday afternoon, and they were concerned. I told the officers that the young woman had canceled her appointment and that I had not seen her for over a week. She was found the next afternoon in the wooded place near campus—she had hanged herself from one of the trees pictured in the photograph she had given me on Friday. The color photograph she had taken and given to me still hangs on my office wall, some twenty-five years later.

Two years later, I had taken a teaching position at a state university in Iowa and maintained a small private practice there with Janice, who was completing her Ph.D., long distance, at Kent State University in Ohio. I received a phone call one afternoon from a colleague at the university, in an academic department other than mine, asking if I was taking new patients. When I said I was, he asked if I would be willing to see him and his wife on a regular basis. Following the initial consultation with the two of them, we agreed that both would do some individual work as well as couple counseling with Janice and me. As we began individual and marriage therapy, we learned that the wife had attempted suicide twice while she and her husband had been together. The first attempt had been a gruesome one, involving scalding-hot tub water and razor blades. The husband had come home early from work to find her and obtained medical attention in time to prevent the suicide. The second and most recent attempt had been within the last two years, following the birth of their first and only child. Their family physician had diagnosed postpartum depression after her barbiturate overdose.

Individual and couple therapy continued for almost a year, becoming more and more sporadic as the two of them appeared to resolve child-rearing differences. She entered graduate school, and her depression lessened. Neither Janice nor I had seen either of them separately or together in therapy for almost two months—it was early winter, I remember—when we received a phone call at our home about ten in the evening. It was my colleague from the university calling to tell us that his wife had committed suicide. He had returned home from teaching an evening class at the university around nine. He found his wife in the garage, the family car running, with the rubber hose connected to its exhaust, feeding fumes into the closed passenger compartment of the automobile. Their daughter was asleep in her room, and the note on her bedside table, written by his wife, said that his daughter had eaten a good supper, had a bedtime story read to her, and had fallen asleep around 8:30 P.M.

Another four years passed, and I was now teaching at a state university in northern Minnesota, as well as training paraprofessional alcohol and substance abuse counselors of the Ojibwa Indian tribe and maintaining a private practice with several colleagues from the university. A former student called me and asked if I would meet with her husband, at his request, at his workplace. He was an editor for the local newspaper, a Vietnam combat veteran, and currently in therapy with a psychiatrist, but he wanted to meet to discuss changing from his current therapist to me. We met in the vending machine room in the basement of the newspaper building at noon. We each drank a cup of coffee, sitting at a small round table in the corner of the room, as he laid out his desire to change therapists, his reasons for wanting to change, and some of the background of his problems and present therapy. He was taking medication for depression, prescribed by his psychiatrist, for which I had no alternative other than talk therapy, which his psychiatrist was already providing. After an hour or so of talking with him, he said he wanted to change therapists and asked if I would be willing to see him. I told him I was not comfortable doing so, for professional and ethical reasons, until he met with his present therapist to tell him he wanted to change therapists and to check out with him the options and need for continued medication. At that point I would then contact his present therapist for the release of appropriate records and information, as well as a professional courtesy. As I left the newspaper building following our meeting, I knew I liked the man very much and looked forward to our working together—I thought I could help him. Two days later, his wife called me again. Her husband had shot himself in the head, sitting at his desk in their den, on Saturday, while she was out shopping. This information would not appear in the local newspaper for a few more days, and she wanted me to know before I read about it.

Although I have written about Marc's suicide before, his loss has nonetheless had a powerful impact on me and my learning how to resolve my feelings of failure as a therapist. Like the newspaper editor, Marc and I were not formally engaged in a client-therapist relationship. Our relationship was that of teacher-student, but it was a meaningful relationship involving closeness. My regret with Marc, as with the newspaper editor, was that I did not become closer to him, and that I did not use my abilities as a therapist to reach out to him more. Also similar to the newspaper editor, Marc killed himself with a gunshot to the head while sitting on a bench in a vacant park of West Germany. Of the four suicides, Marc's is the only funeral I attended. I cannot say whether going to Marc's funeral lessened or increased my sense of loss; a feeling of failure prevailed.

I would be less than honest if I did not also tell you that part of my search for harmony, balance, realization, acceptance, and learning to fail as a therapist has included my own choice to live with my own fears, wounds, hurts, and anger. In Tulsa, Oklahoma, sixteen years ago, I sat in a rocking chair looking at the handgun lying on the bed. Twice I held the gun in my hand, thinking of placing it in my mouth and pulling the trigger. The school of education had been dissolved at the university and, with it, my academic position; I had not been able to find another teaching post, and I had lost confidence in my competence to find another. My world felt out of control and I felt desperate. I was unable to find the end of the string that wound together the strands of my life.

My relationship with Janice was fragile. I pushed her away, and my feelings of closeness toward her receded further and further from expression. I was emotionally barren and distant with her and others as I foundered, trying to renew my confidence and a semblance of control in my life. The fears, pain, wounds, and anger of my childhood, young adulthood, and present station in life made the choice of the gun seem a good one. I thought of my namesake and uncle, Michael, who had taken his life as a young man in the cornfields of rural Wisconsin. What had he thought before drinking the acid? I thought of my failures: my father, the young combat veterans I counseled during Vietnam, my attempt to raise myself from meager lower-class beginnings, the divorce from my first wife, Ross, my flagging career, and Janice. She, and my feelings of connection and closeness to her, was the strand of my life I grasped. Hours later, I picked up the gun, placed it in its shoebox, and returned it to its shelf in the closet.

I have not seen the gun since, and have no idea or desire to know what Janice ever did with it. The more important matter is that this point in my own life has helped me to learn and accept that such a choice was no one else's but mine, and that it was a choice of my individual freedom to live or die. No one could have prevented me from placing the gun in my mouth and pressing the trigger—it was my life, my world, my feelings, my wounds, my fears, my pain, my anger, my choice. Dangling above the deep canyon below, it was my choice alone to let go or to hold on.

Suicide is often described as an angry, pained, and desperate act. But desperation, pain, and anger are also aspects of living. Who is to judge the choice to live a desperate life as better or worse than the choice to end such a life: the survivors, therapists, caregivers, the courts, physicians, the church? For me, blame, guilt, and shame serve no useful purpose in the context of suicide; there is no right or wrong, it is not the success or failure of psychotherapy. Suicide is one of those messy and unpredictable aspects of people—the seaminess of life's messes. It is like the life-taking force of a tumultuous, raging river that sweeps us away in its powerfully chaotic currents. It is a dimension of unknowns, ambiguity, and intense feelings. It happens, it is a choice that some make, and I have had to learn to mourn the losses, recover, rebuild, and move on—the art of resolving my feelings of failure as a therapist.

Patient suicide has also involved my acceptance that some people are broken and cannot be fixed, regardless of my efforts—their fears, hurts, and anger are too great to choose life—and my understanding that psychotherapy cannot heal all wounds. This understanding also includes my accepting individuals' freedom, even the freedom to choose death, and my realizing that choice is both personal and environmental. Some choose drastic and what appear to be impulsive measures to end their lives, while others choose slower means: drug and alcohol abuse, high-stress careers and jobs, unhealthy diets and lifestyles. Psychotherapy cannot prevent, predict, or control such personal choices and environmental factors in the life of another. What it can do is provide a place where the therapist listens and cares deeply, understands and sometimes provides hope, and gives alternative choices that sometimes make a difference—and sometimes do not.

Nonetheless, each time I have encountered the suicide of a student or client I have had to confront my competence as a therapist and issues of control and intimacy. My issues, not those of my student or clients; not the success or failure of psychotherapy, but my feelings of failure. And, many times, my seeking and finding harmony in these areas of being a therapist has caused added conflict. My own father, for example, chose alcohol abuse as the slower path to suicide; here too my conflicts with competence, control, intimacy, and feelings of failure were entangled.

With competence, I always ask whether I missed something obvious; whether there were other choices in my listening, understanding, and responding that may have been effective in preventing the suicide; and what influence my limitations as a therapist may have had on the ultimate choice. The harmonious balance lies somewhere between my feeling as if I have too much influence over a patient and my feeling I have none. Each time I also scuffle with my own moral and ethical issues related to suicide and whether the real issue is a pragmatic, competence one or more closely aligned with my personal philosophical and spiritual beliefs. It is the latter, I think.

In my later years as a therapist, I have come to learn that control is an illusion. I am more drawn to the lack of control, rather than control, I have in the everyday expression of my life, which is often manifest to me in nature: a winter thunderstorm, the infinite beauty of a sunrise or sunset, the individuality in each snowflake and leaf, a hurricane, a rivulet of smoke rising from a chimney, the flow of a river, the choice of a client to commit suicide. I can control or predict none of these, but I know there is order within the disorder and changing patterns within patterns that are sometimes obvious and other times not. Giving up the illusion of control means that I must live with the ambiguity of life and death and not knowing if I have significant influence on someone's life or none at all.

Likewise, especially in matters of suicide, I always question my degree of emotional engagement and personal involvement in the client's life and environment. Was I intimate enough in his or her life and environment, or not? Where was the optimal balance of intimacy in our relationship—did we arrive at that balance in our therapy, could we have changed the ultimate outcome and choice with more time and more intimacy? I know in some instances I have used professional detachment and distance to protect myself from the black hole of clients' despondence and desperation, which can be all-consuming of everything and everyone. At other times, I have become so connected with clients' emotional being that I am able to accept, understand, and empathize with the individual's choices and decisions, even when that choice has been suicide. Either way I am left with my own emotional response, and I struggle to reassess and readjust my internal barometer of intimacy. I have learned the significance of two powerful forces in human relationships: one is power, which, for me, is the ability to influence others; the other is connection, how close or distant I am with someone.

The balance and harmony of these forces are intertwined for me. Having power in a relationship with a client entails our closeness, and closeness entails power; I am most distant from those with whom I have no relationship. But, because I have had some form of relationship, power, and connection with my student, potential client, and clients who committed suicide, the effect on me has always been emotional, creating imbalance and conflict. Death ends a life, not a relationship. I have had to resolve my questions of intimacy and find harmony in the conflict so I could move on and become emotionally reinvolved and personally reengaged with those who followed. The art of it all has been to learn to let go of my end of the rope, turn, and cross the bridge on my journey. As an old man and therapist, however, what I have yet to learn about my end of the rope is when is too soon to let go and when is too long to hang on?

The elders would say, "Gitchi-Manidoo," meaning this is good advice for the young—learning when is too soon to let go and when is too long to hang on to your end of the rope.

Chapter 15

Finding Balance in the Winds

It was a cold wintry night in February, the kind that makes the snow squeak beneath your shoes, as Jim and I drove from Connecticut to Boston to catch a flight to Tucson early the next morning. We were presenting a paper at a professional conference for group workers, but the truth of the matter was that we both needed a little R & R, away from the gloominess of New England's gray winter sky and some time in the warmth of the Arizona sun. We were looking forward to spending time with another male colleague and friend—Edil—whom we had not seen in almost a year and who was also attending the conference as a co-presenter of our paper. Janice was scheduled to attend the conference as a presenter as well, but she had to cancel because of other professional obligations and schedule conflicts. She kidded the three of us about our more personal than professional agenda in going to Tucson, saying that we were acting like we were going deer hunting rather than attending a conference together—knowing the three of us abhor hunting.

She was accurate, however, in that we were going to Arizona to be together. Jim and I made plans to arrive at the conference a day before it began under the guise that we would need the extra time to adjust to the time change. Actually, having lived in Mexico for several years and being fluent in Spanish, Jim had planned a day trip to Mexico for the two of us on our first day in Arizona. And at my persuasion, the three of us had registered for a Native American preconference workshop entitled "Don-Ne-La-We-Ga" (Breathing the Four Winds through the Community of the Circle), also to extend our time together, although Edil would not arrive from Nevada until the night before the workshop.

Jim and I arrived in Tucson to a beautiful blue sky and the warmth of the Arizona desert. We burst into laughter after we checked into the hotel and entered our assigned room. Decorated in a Western motif, our room was audaciously masculine with deer antlers and bull horns hung from every wall in the living area. Through our raucous laughter, we looked at each other and simultaneously said, "Deer hunting!"

We awoke early the next morning, rented a car, and drove out of Tucson through the Arizona desert to the Mexican border town of Nogales. I wanted to stop at the San Xavier Indian Reservation, which was on the way to Nogales. Although aware of the plight of many Native American reservations, I had not prepared myself adequately for the poverty of San Xavier. An old Spanish Mission is located there, and many tourists were wondering about taking pictures. I no longer wanted to be there. Jim and I walked to the Indian Trading Post and I bought a Navajo hair clip for my ponytail and a thumb ring for Janice and we left the reservation in silence. A roadrunner zipped across the highway ahead of us. Because neither Jim nor I had ever seen such a bird, other than its caricature in the Wyle E. Coyote cartoons of our childhood, our focus shifted from the disquiet of the reservation to a discussion of roadrunners and a more optimistic attitude toward our day trip to Mexico.

We parked the car on the United States side of the border and walked into Mexico. Nogales was no better than San Xavier, perhaps worse. We spent several hours in Nogales shopping for Native American rugs and strings of dried chilies, smoking Mexican cigarettes, and eating lunch in a Mexican restaurant the residents of Nogales could not afford to frequent. Despite a delightful interaction with a Spanish-speaking salesclerk, from whom we both purchased beautiful handmade rugs, Jim and I were quiet and somber as we walked back to the border. Jim looked at me with moist eyes and said, "I had forgotten," as a little girl of four or five kept asking us in Spanish to give her a dollar in exchange for a box of Chiclet chewing gum. We talked about San Xavier and Nogales the entire trip back to Tucson, processing our experience and appreciating the renewed awareness that our day trip had jolted into consciousness. I realized again that mine was a very privileged position in life. I reflected on the five years Janice and I had spent in Minnesota teaching paraprofessional counseling and group skills to the Ojibwa, facilitating psychoeducational and counseling groups with them, and the difference they had made in our lives and relationships, and ours in theirs, as a result.

The third member of our "hunting party," Edil, arrived that evening bearing Cuban cigars. We sat about our masculine room, adorned with the horns of dead wild and domesticated animals, smoking cigars and catching up on each other's lives. Although aware of the irony, we joked about deer hunting, laughed together, and enjoyed being in each other's company again. Late that evening, just before going to bed, Jim said he was tired and that he was not sure he was up to the professional content of the next day's eight-hour, preconvention workshop. Edil and I convinced him that we should at least check it out and that if it was taxing or boring, we would all leave politely at the first available recess.

After breakfast, we wondered through the hotel in search of our meeting room, not anxious to actually find it. When we located and entered the large meeting place, a young man was standing at the front of the room with his back turned to its entrance, his single-braided hair extending to the middle of his back, fumbling with artifacts on the table in front of him. Only a few workshop participants had arrived ahead of us, so we found seats together at the rear of the room, close to the exit.

Shortly after, the slightly built young man with braided hair and distinct Native American facial features walked to the rear of the room, near where the three of us sat, carrying his book bag filled with a gourd rattle, a feather, drum, flutes, and other objects. If it was all right with us, he would like to speak from the rear of the room, instead of the front. He removed his white dress shirt and replaced it with a green and black ribbon shirt drawn from his book bag. As the twenty-five group members sat in the straight linear rows facing the front of the prearranged room, the young man asked if we were comfortable with the room, its arrangement, the lighting, and the room temperature. We all quickly rearranged the room into a circle, and the young man smiled as someone fumbled with the light switch and checked the room's thermostat. Perhaps due to my own Native heritage—although socialized white—I was immediately drawn to the young man and captivated by his Indian way.

Michael Tlanusta Garrett said he was twenty-eight years old, from the Eastern Band of Cherokee in North Carolina (the land beneath the rising sun), an assistant professor at the University of North Carolina at Charlotte, and of two hearts: one Irish and one Cherokee. He described a frustrating experience in the airport en route to the conference. A small-town reservation boy, he was uncomfortable in strange surroundings far from his family and home in North Carolina. In the Dallas-Fort Worth Airport, he had nearly decided to cancel his presentation and return home, but he had been raised to be a responsible, good boy and could not shun his obligation to conduct the workshop.

For the next eight hours, I sat fascinated and enthralled with Michael and his use of self in presenting his Native American teachings. Not since I had met Janice twenty-six years earlier had I been so captivated and affected by a person on our first meeting. I kept thinking to myself, "This young man is good; he is really, really good!" It was apparent that Michael truly believed in what he was teaching; his authenticity and genuineness were an extension of his beliefs and who he was as a person; he believed in the process of the group and trusted in the members to find their own places and solutions in the group; and he was confident in his use of self and his intuition to guide the process and his interventions.

Michael did a human factoring exercise early in the workshop based on the Cherokee teachings of the Medicine Wheel and the four winds or four directions. Although I was familiar with the exercise and the content of the four winds, as I, too, am of two hearts (one British and one Ojibwa), I listened intently to Michael. All Native nations, tribes, and clans have their Medicine Wheels, with variations in the totems, fetishes, colors, and animals representing the four winds. Michael instructed us in the importance of harmony and balance in spirit, natural surroundings, body, and mind—known as the four directions or the four winds.

In the Cherokee tradition, the East Wind represents spirit. It is the path of the sun, clarity and honesty, birth and beginning, and unity. The East Wind is a spiritual, heartfelt, sensory, and emotional way of finding personal truths and interpersonal experiences based on a sense of belonging and caring relationships among all things. The color of the East is red, symbolizing the sun, and its totem the eagle, with the ability to soar high and see the world from a wide perspective or to swoop low to the earth and find the smallest details among the grass and overgrowth of the landscape.

The Direction of the South renders a connection with nature. It is the path of peace, adolescence, innocence and renewal, playfulness, fun, and, at times, a sense of feeling vulnerable and being defended. The South Wind is a natural way of youthful innocence based on curiosity, playfulness, and innovation. Personal growth comes from doing and learning through experience and a sense of mastery and exploring interests. Yellow or green is the color of the South Wind, symbolizing the earth and nature, and its totem, the turtle—curious, peaceful, innocent, defended by its impenetrable shell, yet helplessly vulnerable if turned on its back.

The Wind of the West personifies the body and is the path of introspection and strength, adulthood, and self-awareness. The West Wind is a physical way of knowing and learning life's lessons based on the strength that comes when we search and learn from our hearts. Blue or white represents the West Wind, exemplifying water, energy, power and leadership, flow, sustenance and food, cleansing, giving, and connecting and disconnecting. The totem of the West is the bear, also embodying strength and power—strength of the body as well as the force of self-awareness and introspection—and the need at times to retreat and withdraw to its cave, to disconnect from the world for sustenance and cleansing.

The North Wind symbolizes the mind and the path of quiet, trust and purity, old age, and inner calm. The way of the mind is knowing and finding wisdom through openness to experience and learning, with wisdom coming when we are disclosing and accepting. There is a sense of generosity in being open and willing to share with others our life lessons and wisdom. But there is a difference between knowledge and wisdom, in that knowledge is something we take from others, while wisdom is based on our giving, sensitivity, and thinking. The color of the North is black and its totem the hawk or deer, symbolizing the wind itself—sometimes gentle, quiet, unheard and unnoticed, and soothing, but at other times forceful, strong, swift, and overpowering.

As I listened to Michael, my focus turned to his green and black ribbon shirt, the green of his youthful playfulness, innocence, innovation, and fun in the presentation of his teachings—his connection to earth, home, and family in North Carolina—and the black of his inner calm, trust, purity, openness and disclosure—his wisdom at such a young age. One's ribbon shirt and its colors are given to you by your clan or tribe. My mind fleeted back to Connecticut and the white, red, black, and yellow colors of Janice's ribbon shirt and the golden eagle feather given to her by the Ojibwa—the feather she had insisted that I carry with me to Tucson to keep me safe and to protect me, to guide me in my journey. Her strongest wind comes from the direction of the West, the strength and learning that emerges from her heart and her connection with others. The lyrics of an old song came to mind, "Well, I'm older now and still riding against the wind, against the wind. . . . Like cowboys riding against the wind . . . against the wind . . . I guess I lost my way. . . . Searching for shelter against the wind." And, I thought to myself, "Am I still this out of balance and harmony? Deer hunting? Were Jim, Edil, and I seeking the path of quiet inner calm, openness and acceptance, sharing and giving—the totem of the deer and wisdom?"

The winds of my own life were in turmoil and at great odds; I was always feeling their force at my face and never at my back. Professionally, I was the disconnected bear of the West Wind, withdrawn from students, peers, and the groups I taught or facilitated for reasons of self-protection, cleansing, and introspection, and to rethink professional priorities. Personally, but only with people closest to me, I was walking the path of the deer and willing to accept and disclose the wisdom of the North Wind's experience and learning. Nevertheless, I was out of balance and harmony in my life; my professional and personal winds at odds with one another. But, young Michael Tlanusta Garrett, his teachings, and his workshop were about to change that.

After his presentation of the four winds, Michael asked the workshop participants to place themselves physically in the part of the meeting room that literally represented one of the four directions of east, south, west, and north that best typified their honest perception of their own direction in life. "Which of the four winds best symbolizes where you are in your life right now, not where you want to be, but where you are right now? That's the part of the room I want you to go to," Michael said. I wanted desperately to place myself in the

West (the bear safely disconnected in his cave) but I honestly felt my direction in life was East. Somewhat assured in knowing that, in Native tradition, opposing winds complement one another, North-South and East-West, I walked hesitantly to the part of the room opposite where I wanted to place myself—the East rather than the West—still conflicted and off balance, and stood with others who stood there. "Well, I'm older now and still riding against the wind, against the wind. . . . Like cowboys riding against the wind . . . against the wind." Michael told us the people with whom we had clustered were now our clan, and that we would be doing small-group exercises with them during the rest of the workshop. Edil stood in the North and Jim in the South. As I looked at them across the room, I thought, "I didn't come here to spend my time with a bunch of strangers, I came here to be with Jim and Edil."

It was lunchtime, and Michael instructed us to eat our noontime meal with our clans, to get to know one another. Resisting the group process and the leader's instructions, Edil, Jim, and I picked up our box lunches from the table near the hotel's swimming pool and found a quiet place in the shade to share our meal—just the three of us, choosing the friendship and spirituality of our own established clan over the new clans to which we had been assigned. After lunch, Michael again instructed the workshop participants to break out into our respective clans, giving each a specific exercise to perform. I reluctantly sought out my clan members, who, ironically, were sitting in the same place where Jim, Edil, and I had eaten lunch together. As I joined the group, I could sense the tension. They were angry, upset that I had not followed instructions and had not eaten lunch with them, demanding to know who I was, why I had chosen to place myself in the East, and how I was spiritual. Responding initially from the disconnection and self-protective strength of my West Wind, I smiled and told them I did not think their reaction to me was very spiritual. Then, unexpectedly, my eyes filled with tears and my lower lip began to quiver slightly. My voice was shaky and caught in my throat as I said, "Look, I didn't come here to be with you folks. I came here to be with the people I love because we live in different parts of the country now and I miss them. They are my real clan, they are the people with whom I share a sense of belonging and caring relationships; they are the ones with whom I feel spiritual."

My clan sat in silence for some time, until someone said, "Thank you, Michael, thank you for being in our clan." The clarity of my heartfelt emotional honesty confirmed for me that I was indeed trying to follow the path of the sun and the East Wind. The energy of the group changed, and we went about completing the exercise that Michael had assigned to us: sharing and discussing the spirituality of life and in our life experiences.

Throughout the day, Michael continued to share himself and his Native traditions and teachings. He talked of the sacredness of personal, interpersonal, and environmental space; of interference and noninterference; of gifts and totems; of clearing and cleansing; and of balance and harmony among the winds. He shared with us the power of his feather and medicine bag, but he was quick to acknowledge that not all of one's power and medicine should be given to others, and that we must keep some of it to and for ourselves. He played his gourd rattle and drum as members of the workshop spoke of their lives and experiences, respectfully holding his feather in their hands. He cleansed and cleared our minds with the smoke of burning sage and cedar cradled in a concave seashell from North Carolina. He taught us to respect the community of the talking circle, always asking permission to enter its shape from the East and walking to one's place in a clockwise direction. He sang for us the impatience of a song sung by a young Native man and contrasted that with singing the same song with the slow, deliberate patience and wisdom of an old Native man. He told us of the honor and respect conveyed by calling an elder "old man" or "old woman." With his flutes, he played a musical dialogue between a young Native boy and his grandfather, using his two different flutes to convey the voices of the boy and his grandfather—as tears streamed the cheeks of several workshop members. He ended the workshop by giving each of us an acorn from a small, leather bag—while we stood holding hands in the community of the circle—and asked that each of us plant it when we returned to our homes.

From Michael's workshop and his leadership, I realized it was time for me to come out of my cave. I learned to share again with others my openness and willingness to disclose with them my life lessons and heartfelt emotions: the openness and acceptance that comes from the strength of knowing myself, of believing in the process of groups, of following the restored balance and harmony in the winds of my life, and of trusting in my own sense and use of self as a healing power in my leadership of groups.

Jim, Edil, and I were to spend more time with Michael following the preconference workshop. We met again at several social functions during the conference, we talked of serious matters while sitting in the warmth of the Arizona sun, we laughed and had fun together, and we shared the spirituality of a new clan and family, eating several meals together. Michael attended our paper presentation at the conference, to which I took Janice's golden eagle feather enclosed in its red container, removing it from its casing and placing it on a table, depicting her and her presence with us, as Edil, Jim, and I gave our presentation. Afterward, Michael said, "I knew it was something sacred you carried in the red holder." Later that evening, as we walked to our rooms at the end of the day, Michael asked me if I would be his uncle. I replied by saying that I did not know if I was worthy of being his uncle. Michael responded, "Old man, the question is whether I am worthy of being your nephew." I turned my face toward the darkness, hiding the tears that were filling my eyes. I waited for several moments, as Michael and I continued to walk, to gather myself and clear the choked feeling from my throat, before I said, "Yes, Michael, I would be honored to have you as my nephew."

Edil left early the following morning, before Jim and I. After a long and teary-eyed embrace, I watched Edil walk down the balcony toward the hotel lobby and his waiting taxi—and the North Wind that would carry him home to Nevada. He never looked back and I knew why. Jim and I were to fly back to Boston, then driving to Connecticut, from where Jim would follow the South Wind to North Carolina. He was living there now, caring for his elderly mother after the death of his father the year before. Ironically, Jim and Michael lived only an hour's drive from one another in North Carolina.

In the Tucson airport, an elderly Native man—a security guard—pulled me aside in the boarding area for our flight near the luggage conveyor belt and metal detector, "Random check. Would you open your bag for me please?" I unzipped my carry-on bag and handed it to him. Looking into the small piece of luggage, the first thing he found was the red case holding the eagle feather. He carefully lifted the container from the bag, "What is this? Your feather?"

"Yes, it is my feather."

He gingerly returned the red holder and its feather to the luggage, rezipped it, and handed it back to me, saying, "A good day."

Uncertain if this was a statement or a question, I replied, "Yes. Yes it is, old man. A good day."

For almost three years before the Tucson conference, the directions and winds of my own life were not in balance. For the most part, I was aware of how out of balance I was. I was not available to clients and students, I withdrew into myself and revealed very little to others about my thoughts or feelings—I was disconnected, like the bear of the West who hibernates in its cave for sustenance and cleansing. I kept a noninterfering distance from others and maintained solid personal and professional boundaries between myself and others. To be sure, much of this behavior was self-preserving, but I was also aware of the harm I could cause others in the absence of such boundaries and disconnection. Gradually, I have come out of my cave, found renewed balance in my life, and begun to reconnect with myself and others, due considerably to the person of Michael Tlanusta Garrett and the disclosing and accepting wisdom of his North Wind as well as his playful nature.

The use of self in therapy reflects an underlying philosophical belief about the person of the therapist or group leader. It is the therapists' ability to use themselves as a healing tool to help another—something I had lost during my time of imbalance and lack of harmony in my life. The therapist's use of self in psychotherapy is a matter of balance and harmony among mind, body, spirit, and natural surroundings—the balance and harmony of both the group leader and the members. If the therapist has found balance in the winds of his or her own life, I believe the self may be used in a self-revealing, flexible, and helpful manner through the flow and exchange between the other's boundaries of self. In the absence of such balance, however, the group leader's use of self may indeed become self-serving, narcissistic, interfering, and potentially harmful to the members.

In the years before Michael's workshop, I had lost my balance, my belief in groups, and belief in myself as a group leader. I had become very technical and safe in my group leadership, following the prescribed guidelines, norms, and stages of group development and group work. I did everything right and by the book, but there was no sense of who I was as a person in the process or in interaction with my students and group members. Observing Michael facilitate his group workshop in Tucson, I felt again the power and effectiveness of the leader's use of self as a healing tool. Michael's own harmony, balance, and self-disclosure renewed my faith in group process and the leader's use of self as a powerful healing force.

Thus, in balance with the four winds, I believe the therapist intuitively knows when and how much interference, self-revealing, and use of self are appropriate and helpful to a client. I also believe the in-balance group leader is capable of knowing and can sense how in or out of balance group members may be and adjusts his or her use of self accordingly. With members who are markedly out of balance, the in-balance leader knows there is a need to maintain stricter, stronger boundaries between himself or herself and group members and that less or no self-revealing and use of self by the leader are appropriate. As a noteworthy aside, Michael did not interact with me directly at all during the course of the workshop itself. He and I both knew I was struggling to regain my balance and harmony, and his response to me—and rightly so—was one of noninterference.

A bigger problem ensues, however, for which I have only a tentative answer, when group leaders themselves do not have the self-awareness to know when their own harmony is out of balance. For many group leaders—by their own choosing or their inability to know themselves; the sacredness of the self; the sacredness of personal, interpersonal, and environmental space; of gifts and totems; of cleansing and clearing; and of balance and harmony among the four winds—the use of self in groups is not appropriate. In this instance, I believe closed and distant leader-member relationships are required as is maintaining well-defined boundaries.

Although I had come to such an out-of-harmony place in my own life and group leadership, I was aware of my imbalance, my closed and distant relationships, and the reasons for them. But Michael's teachings, modeling, and use of self in his group workshop restored my belief in groups and renewed my efforts to find balance and harmony in the four winds of my own life and group leadership.

As I reflected on this experience, I also recalled something I had written some years ago about the effectiveness of group process and leadership. Something I had lost, but have since rediscovered thanks to Michael's group workshop and his healing leadership:

> Alas, the "process" of groups remains elusive and nebulous. No matter what the structure, number or member

composition, consistency of leader behavior and group procedures, or predictable group stages that unfold—each group is different. Although this aspect provides for ambiguity and frustration at times, it also makes each group different and exciting. . . . I still recall my first graduate course in group process. I was eager to learn "how" to be an effective, productive group member and, "someday," to become an effective group leader. The very first thing the professor, who later became my "group mentor," said to the class was, "The single most important factors in facilitating an effective group are the leader's authenticity and genuineness and the leader's belief in groups. As a leader, if you are not who you are, and if you do not believe that groups affect people and their lives, then the groups you facilitate will not be effective." . . . I now trust in myself and group members that the process will be an expression of our realness in interaction with others and that the effect will be meaningful for all of us. I do not know of anyone who has ever demonstrated conclusively the effectiveness of group therapy, or individual therapy for that matter. One develops a belief in group process and its effects by experiencing them as a group member or leader, not by studying, quantifying, and measuring discrete group variables. One creates an effective group by expressing one's realness and beliefs in interaction with others. How does one evaluate and measure such expressions? . . . For her graduation, a student who had been a member of my graduate-level group courses gave me a copy of [the children's book] *The Polar Express* and a silver bell from Santa's sleigh. The last page of *The Polar Express* reads, "At one time most of my friends could hear the bell, but as the years passed, it fell silent for all of them. . . . Though I have grown old[er], the bell still rings for me as it does for all who truly believe."

I also wrote earlier that I believe the profession of psychotherapy has changed so dramatically over the past twenty-six years that, among many professionals of our trade, group leaders' own self-knowledge or self-awareness no longer seems to be needed. For these colleagues among us, I am almost certain their reaction to my suggestions for the group leader's use of self and disclosure in groups, let alone such Native traditions and teachings as the four directions and winds, will be strong objection, if not negativity, citing chapter and verse the guidelines for professional ethics and standards, dual relationships, and the risks and potential harmful consequences of self-disclosure by group leaders and therapists. What a loss of such a powerful and healing therapeutic tool in the process of groups—the person of the group leader.

None of us was ready for the conference in Arizona to end. Standing on the hotel veranda the last night, we embraced, called one another brother, uncle, nephew, and family, and said goodbye to Michael. We knew we would be together again—sometime, somewhere—all my life's a circle. Even though Michael and Janice had not met one another yet, our circle was strong and our sense of self—through the flow and exchange between the other's boundaries of self—complete: Edil following the quiet path of the North Wind's knowledge and wisdom, Jim and Michael connected with Nature and walking the path of peace—having fun—in the Wind of the South, Janice flowing with the power of rivers in the West Wind of her heart and connections with others, and I . . . I am seeking personal truth in the path of the sun and the East Wind.

I sat quietly in the airplane, listening to the soft pulse of a Native heart and the distant tone of a sleigh bell, as Jim and

I flew back to Boston, riding the strong East Wind home to the land beneath the rising sun, holding Janice's golden eagle feather gently in my lap—the feather a symbol of her own life harmony shared with me these many years. Well, I'm older now and riding with the winds . . . riding with the winds: "Don-Ne-La-We-Ga."

— Edutsi

Chapter 16

Pine Island

"Don't dodder by the river, Michael, don't hang over the railing of the bridge, don't you even go near the water. You hear me?"

"I won't, Mom. Okay, Mom. I won't, Mom. Yeah, I hear you, Mom." I was never sure if it was her own fear of the water I was dealing with, or her fear for me. Maybe some of both. Every year, though, some kid would be pulled from the river by Zeke, the local gas station attendant at the corner Standard Service Station, right next to the river's east-end bridge and dam, or drown if Zeke didn't get there in time. There were all kinds of plaques and awards—hanging on the grimy wall behind the even greasier counter inside the service station—right next to a filmy paned window overlooking the river—given to Zeke by the Lion's Club, the Jaycees, the Rotary Club, the town mayor, the Fire and Police Department (and one from the state's governor) for his bravery in rescuing kids from the river. Most people said Zeke never washed your windshield or checked your oil because he wouldn't leave his watch of the river for any longer than it him took to pump a few gallons of gas.

My boyhood town was an island town, surrounded by the Grand River—and grand it was, although the town itself wasn't much by the time I came along. Just a small town of forty-five hundred folks; most of whom worked in the car factories in Lansing, ten miles north on route 99, and those who were still trying to farm the worn-out muck fields. In the olden days, though, the town had also been grand, from the stories I heard and the pictures I saw, anyway. It was a place of mineral baths, luxurious hotels, and paddleboats on the river; people came from all over the world to heal themselves in the hot baths of the natural springs and to drink the magical water. Before that it had been a commercial center for gristmills and shipping grain on the river and the railroads.

As a kid, I wished I had lived in those earlier times; I loved the river and the island town it created, but it didn't offer much for me in my time there. Taverns—*beer gartens* (a German influence) we called them—were located on every street corner (except for the corner with Zeke's Standard Station), replacing all the old, opulent hotels that had been torn down or had burned down over the years. The mineral baths were all gone, and only one gazebo-like stone drinking fountain—flowing continuously with spring water—remained in front of Horner's Woolen Mill.

As I look back on my boyhood and my time in the small, Midwest river town of my youth, it is a time and place of fond memories—and some not so fond memories—in which I was popular, well-known, and excelled athletically and academically. But I also knew at a young age that it was a place I would one day leave, although I have never forgotten that small island or its grand river.

Despite my mother's admonitions, I always loitered by the river on my walk to school and dangled over the bridge railing, although the number of bridges I crossed on my way to school increased from my elementary to high school days. It was the west-end bridge I traversed daily while in elementary and junior high school, and both the west- and east-end bridges by the time I was in high school. Dams were located near each of the bridges, built in the 1940s to prevent the reoccurrence of the 1939 flood that had almost destroyed the town.

Nevertheless, during heavy rain or snow the river ran deep and fast. It hardly ever froze over entirely and, even if it did, the ice was a thin, transparent sheet with flowing water visible through it. With my feet off the sidewalk a foot or so and my elbows and forearms supporting me on the concrete railing of the bridge, I would peer over its edge and watch, fascinated, as the water raced itself to the huge culvert openings that ran beneath the bridge and roadway, rampaging against itself and the bridge's cement steles, reinforced with steel, spraying mist and splats of water in my face. Whoever, or whatever, encountered that rampaging element would not survive its crushing turbulence or the even greater melee between the river and the dam on the other side of the bridge. Just to insure my conclusion was accurate, I would often toss something into the river—a pencil stub, a piece of notebook paper, a gum wrapper, a discarded bottle cap—hurriedly cross the roadway over the bridge and the adjoining parking lot next to Miller's Ice Cream Parlor, and gawk at the rapids storming over the damn. Not once did I ever see again any of the objects I sacrificed to the river.

I respected the river and its power, but I didn't fear it. That was my mom's feeling, I realized years later, not mine. I knew it could be a life-taking force; but it also gave me a sense of comfort, security, and stability. It was always there and never went away, it was strong, it demanded respect, it wouldn't mess with you unless you messed with it—or didn't show it reverence—and it could be calm and peaceful, despite its ability to rage.

In the summer, my boyhood chums and I would trade bubble-gum baseball cards at Applebee's bait and swap-shop for night crawlers and grubs and fish for pike off the island point. I never told mom about our summer fishing on the river, and my buddies took home with them any fish we caught. My father also liked to take me with him after dark in the summer evenings to fish for bullhead (some people call them catfish) from the abandoned railroad trestle over the river; so he could drink beer away from my mom's constant hounding and nagging about his drinking. We would sit together with our legs hanging over the edge of the railroad ties—with big, dangerous spaces between them, I thought as a kid—our long cane fishing poles extending out above the water. I loved sitting there with Dad, in the dim glow of the kerosene lantern, waiting for a nibble on our lines or for the white-topped bobber to disappear beneath the surface of the water. He drank his beer, sometimes whiskey, too, and I listened to him talk about his adventures as a Screaming Eagle paratrooper in World War II.

He talked of the battles he had fought, the men he had killed and seen killed, his jumping from airplanes, his silver star with two oak-leaf clusters, his crossing of the Rhine River, in Holland, in a small raft with three other men—and their capture of thirty-two German soldiers without firing a single shot. As a young boy, sitting with him on the trestle and listening to his "constant war stories"—as mom called them—I would think to myself, and told him the same when I was a

He stopped by our house one summer afternoon, visibly shaken and emotionally distressed. His small sailboat had capsized in heavy winds on the Sound, with two others aboard. They were rescued by a passing fishing boat, but one of the crew had been trapped in an air pocket beneath the boat's hull and it was only with much difficulty that she had been coaxed to the water's surface and the awaiting rescuers.

A few days later, Jim again stopped by our house and told Janice and me that he was going to give up sailing. An hour or so later, as he was about to leave, Janice leaned over to him and whispered in his ear, "Jim, don't give up sailing, just buy a bigger boat." The next Saturday morning, Jim came by to see us again, and asked if I would go with him to look at a thirty-foot sailboat he had found advertised in the newspaper. We drove the thirty-two miles to Long Island Sound, met the man who owned the boat, took his dinghy out to its mooring, and went for a sail. The boat had some structural problems, so Jim and I walked around the marina docks looking for boats for sale and enjoyed the sea breeze together on that warm, sunny afternoon. Jim found the boat he was to buy that same afternoon, and we returned inland.

I talked nonstop to Janice for hours after I got home, about the boats moored in the marina, the sea breeze flowing over the Sound, the sun's reflection off the ocean's surface, the small mariner's bar where Jim and I ate lunch—I talked about the water.

I canceled plans to build the barn, and three weeks later used the money lent to me by Jim, with his blessing and encouragement, to buy our own sloop from one of Janice's co-workers at the university. On the twelfth of August, 1999, I found the place of water in my life once again—we moored our boat at Pine Island. It's a small marina in Groton, Connecticut, near the university's Avery Point campus, New London's shipyard and the building place of the *Seawolf* submarine, the U.S. Coast Guard Academy, and the Naval submarine base. The quaint New England marina, tucked among pine trees and the small cove of Pine Island, is owned and operated by three young men in their late twenties or early thirties who have been friends since their own boyhood: Pete, Jeff, and Rick. Their love for the sea, boats, doing what they do, and for each other is obvious to those who take the time to notice.

Of course, it's a business for Jeff, Rick, and Pete, and their means of livelihood, but they have never laughed at or criticized our beginners' mistakes and ignorance of sailing. Their comment, and those of the old salts at the marina, has always been, "Everyone has to begin somewhere." Pine Island is a small and welcoming place where we can connect to the water, a place of laid-back comfort and slow pace (due to these same characteristics in Pete, Jeff, and Rick, I think), a place where we choose to be.

Initially, though, Pine Island and the sea stirred the old warnings and cautions of my mother: "Don't dodder by the river, Michael, don't hang over the railing of the bridge, don't you even go near the water. You hear me?" Although everyone has to begin somewhere, Pine Island wasn't a beginning place for me. The marina's cove and Long Island Sound reminded me of my hometown island and the waters of my childhood memories. When I first clambered aboard our sailboat—legs visibly shaking and unsteady—I held tightly to every lifeline and piece of rigging I could find. I never ventured forward to her bow—I just sat quietly in the safety of the boat's cockpit or below deck in the cabin. I was fearful of taking our own dinghy from the dock to our boat's mooring, and I always timed our arrival at the marina so that we could catch the launch—piloted by an experienced boater—that shuttled us between the dock and our boat.

As the summer wore on and I spent more and more time aboard our boat at Pine Island, the fears and warnings of my mother faded and lifted from my heart. I grew my sea legs, walking confidently and nimbly fore and aft on the sloop's deck, and the awe and beauty of the sea restored my fascination with the water. Comfort, harmony, and balance washed over my soul when I was on the water. Merely gazing at the sea while I stood on the docks of the marina provided a renewed sense of security and stability to my life.

Near the end of our first sailing season, Janice and I awoke aboard the boat to sunny skies and a light wind. We had taken the sloop into the Sound several times before, using only the foresail. We decided to go out for what might be our last sail of the year, as the late autumn winds and seas were becoming more unpredictable and turbulent. As we left the channel, I raised the foresail and Janice guided us into the Sound, the wind at our back. I spotted for lobster pots and we sped into deeper water, heeling strongly to port but not realizing, at first, that the winds had come up quickly and changed direction. Trying to tack, we jibed instead, and turned into the wind. The swells were three to four feet—huge in our novice experience—and I suggested it might be a good idea to head back to the marina.

Janice handled the boat masterfully and said in a calm voice, "Michael, I think you should go below and get the life jackets." At this I lost all composure. I hurriedly tried to get into my personal flotation device, only making matters worse as the straps and buckles became more and more twisted and confused. Janice calmly slipped into hers, holding the helm gently with her knee. All I could think about was all those objects I had thrown from the bridge of my small island town into the Grand River's strong and rapid currents, never to see them surface again.

I became disoriented, not knowing which direction was which or where the marina lay. I couldn't tell one buoy from another and said to Janice, "Where are we? We're not moving forward at all!" She reassured me that we were indeed making progress under sail, that all would be well, and that we were okay. Nevertheless, she agreed to let me lower the foresail and motor the remaining way back to Pine Island. We tied up to our mooring—negotiating into a strong northerly wind—like a couple of seasoned old salts, and I breathed a sigh of relief that I had not been swept away like a bottle cap, gum wrapper, piece of notebook paper, or pencil stub by the currents of the sea—never to surface again. Safely moored at Pine Island, I thought, "Well, I just might recover from my mother after all."

For most of my twenty-six years with Janice I have been a "homebody," not wanting to go far from home or to become involved in outside activities. Remember, I was going to build a landlocked, post-and-beam barn in my driveway; I wasn't thinking sailboat. It's hard, now, to think I lived only thirty miles from the sea for ten years, and that I never went there until that summer. When our youngest daughter visited us five years ago, she asked, "Do you live near the ocean? I can smell it."

"Yeah, we're pretty close," I said, "But I can't smell it." Now I can't stop smelling it, and Janice had to ask me to slow down a bit and let her catch up to the drastic change in my behavior; I want to go to Pine Island, to the sea, and to our sailboat all the time.

It's sad for me to pull our boat and put her up on ways for the winter, despite my once fearful, questioning, doubtful times with the water. I go to Pine Island nearly every week in the wintertime and check on her. I always walk down on the docks and sit for a while, my legs dangling over the edge, if the day is warm enough and the breeze not too bone-chilling. Even on cold days, I still walk down to the dock and look at the water, the wind and mist blowing in my face, and I dodder for a while. I'm coming to realize that Pine Island and the sea are different from the small island town of my youth and the waters of its river. Or, maybe it's me who is finally different.

Janice gave me a small refrigerator magnet for my birthday recently. I have it on the fridge door, right next to a picture of our sailboat. Its inscription says, "The cure for anything is saltwater, sweat, tears, or the sea." She's right, you know. Pine Island is a place of calm and peace, a place of comfort, security, and stability. The sea is always there and never goes away; it's strong and demands respect, and it won't mess with you unless you mess with it—or don't show it reverence. But, it's not the island and waters of my boyhood. It's Pine Island; it's sitting placidly and quietly together in the sailboat's cockpit—talking late into the night; it's being rocked to sleep together in the V berth of the sloop's cabin; it's learning to sail together in strong winds and rough seas; it's the cure for anything in the midst of a life-taking force and its rage; it's finding your old man in the sea.

References

Arnold, M. 1822–1888. *The Forsaken Merman,* 1849. In *The Oxford Dictionary of Quotations 1980,* 3rd ed., p. 13. Oxford, England: Oxford University Press.

Atwood, M. 1996. *Alias Grace.* New York: Anchor Books/Doubleday.

Bunnel, Dewey (songwriter). 1975. "Tin Man." From America, *History: Greatest Hits,* 1987. New York: Warner Brothers Records.

Canning, G. 1770–1827. *House of Commons,* 1802. In *The Oxford Dictionary of Quotations 1980,* 3rd ed., p. 130. Oxford, England: Oxford University Press.

Chapin, H., F. Kewley, S. Chapin (producers), and H. Chapin (songwriter). 1976. "Cat's in the Cradle." From *Harry Chapin: Greatest Stories Live* (Compact disc recording No. 6003-2). New York: Elektra/Asylum Records.

Coles, R. 1993. "When Earnest Volunteers are Sorely Tested." *The Chronicle of Higher Education* 34 (May 5): A52.

Engel, R. 1945. "The Incredible Patrol." *Life* (January 15): 75–83.

Evans, N. 1995. *The Horse Whisperer.* New York: Delacorte Press.

Freud, S. 1929. *Introductory Lectures on Psychotherapy.* London: Allen-Unwin.

Getman, J. 1992. *In the Company of Scholars: The Struggle for the Soul of Higher Education.* Austin: University of Texas Press.

Goleman, D. 1995. *Emotional Intelligence.* New York: Bantam Books.

Haley, J. 1996. *Learning and Teaching Therapy.* New York: The Guilford Press.

Leeson, T. 1994. "The Unspecifiable Eloquence of Rivers." *The Chronicle of Higher Education* XL: B2.